Technology in Media

Copyright 2015

Ed Morawski

Technology in Media

A Writer's Resource

Foreword

Whether you're an amateur first time writer or a professional - do you want your stories to be realistic? As a consumer of books, movies, and television we certainly do. Nothing ruins a plot more for us than reading or seeing something completely wrong or unrealistic or worst of all - impossible.

Having been in the military and then in the security and alarm business since 1973, I am acutely aware when a writer doesn't know what they're talking about.

Example: A character uses a cigarette lighter to set off a fire sprinkler system thereby flooding an entire building.

Sorry - it just doesn't work that way. While one could set off ONE sprinkler head by climbing up to it on a ladder - only that specific sprinkler goes off - not the entire building like in the movies.

I got so tired of reading books and seeing films with glaring errors about technology I decided to write this resource for authors. So instead of using an erroneous plot device, arm yourself with the facts and be clever - and that will set you apart!

Now we don't intend to demean anyone. Many of you will know all or some of this, many of you will not. The intent here is two fold:

1) to help by providing an insider's knowledge of the subjects.

2) to organize research material in one handy guide to save time.

This guide is not intended as an in depth technical course of these specific technologies, if you want details you can further explore Google. Instead it presents real world capabilities, structured so you can go directly to the subject matter you need. But we encourage you to skip around or read the entire book since hopefully it may give you some inspiration and new ideas. And it may even provide information you didn't know you wanted!

Table of Contents

Here are some of the subjects we will cover:

Burglar Alarms

So you want your character to break into some business or building (or home) for some reason. We often laugh when we read or see these exploits - like a guy breaks into a veterinary clinic to patch up a knife wound - with nary a care in the world. He just breaks the glass, no alarm, no problem. But did you know that about 90% of businesses have alarms? Especially those that have any kind of drugs or medical supplies. They couldn't get insurance if they didn't. Nearly every business from auto repair to dry cleaners to scrap and junk yards (yes that scrap is like gold) have alarms. It's a rare place of business of any kind that doesn't have an alarm.

So be realistic and assume there's going to be an alarm system and the easiest way to tell is that the alarm company is going to place their stickers or signs everywhere because it's good advertising - and deterrent. Your character is either going to have to defeat the alarm system or think of another way. Don't gloss over this - or panic - this is an opportunity to make your story or script interesting. In fact there is so much 'meat' in alarms and security systems you can have a field day representing them correctly.

First thing to consider is that the people who design and manufacture alarm systems are not stupid; they know every trick and how to counteract them. As in any other system, cost and time are the bigger factors in defeating it. The cost factor goes hand in hand with the time factor. The lower the cost of the system (mostly residential types), the faster it can be defeated. If one buys a cheap alarm system, they will get less protection and a system easier to defeat. On the other hand, given enough time and resources one can defeat almost anything. Modern alarm systems balance these two factors quite well.

In order to be aware of or exploit the weaknesses of a system, you need to understand the system. With that in mind we will explore and explain each component of alarms and security systems. Perhaps first we should explain the terms 'alarm' and 'security' as used in this book.

'Alarm' will be used to designate an intrusion system designed to deter and detect burglars.

'Security' on the other hand will describe any other system designed to detect, deter, control, and document intruders or unauthorized persons. Some examples of these security systems are:

Video Surveillance (CCTV, digital video, DVRs, etc.)

Card Access (key cards, card keys, access cards, etc.)

Biometric Identity Systems (fingerprint and retinal scan)

Metal Detectors

Human Security

We will also explain a critical part of every alarm system - the Central Monitoring Station - the place your actual alarm signal goes for processing and handling.

With the above in mind, we will cover each system and each component, detailing how it works, its strengths and weaknesses, and potential ways to bypass or defeat it.

Before we start however, you need to get some things out of your head - like everything you've ever seen in a movie or on television! It extremely rare to see any movie or TV show that actually portrays an alarm or security system accurately. In fact, security professionals always get a good laugh at what they see on the silver screen. Some scenarios are so ludicrous it's astounding how even uninformed people could fall for them. But that's Hollywood and the reasons they do what they do are strictly visual. I worked closely with producers, directors, and set decorators on quite a few movies and they are not the least bit interested in reality- only how something looks on screen (or they had no research budget).

One case in point- how many times have you seen actors slide, swipe, or insert access key cards when trying to get through a high security door? The truth is, the real security industry abandoned that technology twenty years ago. These days, 99% of card readers are of the 'proximity' type; which means the card just has to be held within four inches of the reader. Modern readers are contactless and can even read through clothes, purses and briefcases. Although I have pointed this fact out to numerous movie production people, they don't want the actual product because they don't 'look cool'. Movie people think it looks a lot better if the actor has to do something - like sliding a card through a reader.

Another great myth is that fire sprinkler system. Again, how many times have you seen a movie where the actor lights a match and sets off every sprinkler in the building? In reality only the specific sprinkler head which senses the fire – the exact one where the match is being held - will discharge water. But the truth just doesn't look good or advance the story.

So get all that Hollywood baloney out of your mind and we'll explain how alarms really work! The fact is, although some individual components of alarms and security systems do have weaknesses, when they are put together in a complete system those potential weaknesses are for the most part counteracted. The truth is, a modern alarm system is extremely hard to defeat.

While this book won't make your movie experience more enjoyable, it will give you plenty of ammunition to argue with your friends and it will help make your story so much more interesting.

The Alarm System

An alarm system consists of many individual pieces which are designed to work together as an intrusion detection system. Notice the term: 'detection' – an alarm system can only detect burglars, it can't stop them or capture them- an important point to keep in mind.

The typical alarm system consists of a control panel (which usually includes a method of communication), a keypad to arm and disarm it, detection devices (door contacts and motion detectors), and a sounder such as a bell or siren. These are parts you are probably somewhat familiar with, but there are many more devices which manage the alarm and are designed to complete the overall detection system.

The Control Panel

Years ago, control panels were very crude and simple (an important point depending in which era your story is set); sometimes consisting of only a switch and a latching relay. When the owner entered his business the alarm signaled the monitoring station and the operators there expected a phone call wherein the owner would provide a code word identifying themselves. As more and more alarms were installed the alarm control was provided an on/off switch and as long as the alarm was within the scheduled time provide by the owner no response was initiated.

Along about the 1990's microprocessors changed all that and now control panels are extremely sophisticated and intelligent. In fact, control panels have so many features that only a fraction of them are actually used on by most people.

The control panel serves as the brains of the alarm. It monitors the keypad and the detection devices and makes 'if-then' decisions based on programming. Alarm control panel programs can be quite complex and perform many functions such as managing communications, entry & exit delays, monitoring the integrity of all the wiring, storing user PINs and activity- as well as handling all different types of alarm events. Programs can easily run into as many as 500 entries and as a result are often entered through a laptop or by remote download.

Control panels manage many more functions than just the burglar detection. They contain a power supply including a backup battery and charger. They monitor the actual wires in your system to maintain integrity. They manage the communications- including dialing multiple numbers repeated times until the signal gets through. Beyond these functions, the control panel also maintains the audible warnings (bells, sirens, voice, etc.), entry / exit delay (which we'll explain shortly, and remembers the PIN numbers or keypad combinations for multiple users.

Another responsibility of the control panel is backup power. All systems contain at least one standby battery which is usually capable of running the system at full efficiency for at least 4 to 24 hours and often as long as 72 hours.

Besides just sounding a bell or siren locally, the control panel is also responsible for transmitting the actual alarm signal to the monitoring station. Very few, if any, police departments these days will receive alarms directly - they are just too busy. 99.9 % of all alarms go to a private central monitoring station, which decodes the alarm signals and then human operators take the appropriate action: notify the police and the customer.

Controls panels transmit much more than just alarm signals. They can log power loss, when the system is armed or disarmed, and which user did it. This last feature can be invaluable to managers and owners to have an audit trail of their employees.

The system usually communicates to the central monitoring station by phone lines. Residences can use the phone line already there, but many alarm companies require businesses install a dedicated phone line just for the alarm. This is not bad advice. Although it increases the total monthly cost, a dedicated line reduces the chance the alarm control won't be able to get through to the central station. If the intrusion system can't dial out and deliver the alarm message, the central station won't be aware of an alarm condition- another important point.

Newer alarm systems (and more advanced monitoring companies) now offer 'internet' monitoring. Instead of the traditional phone line, they use broadband Internet access such as DSL or cable. Some systems continuously monitor the condition of the line by continuously sending test messages to the monitoring company's computers and can warn if the connection is lost. These are highly secure because of their speed and security. Internet communication is two-way - the alarm monitoring company can actually detect if the customer's panel is not replying because it is off-line.

The latest trend is GSM cellular communication. Alarm manufacturers have realized many people no longer have traditional land line phone lines so they have begun to rapidly deploy cellular communications. Cellular has distinct advantages and disadvantages as you will see.

When wired (internet or phone) communication is used, the phone line is the weak link and must be protected from cutting. This is something to be especially aware of in residential applications. If the phone line exposed, then burglars can easily cut it. This is one of the primary weaknesses of the modern alarm system - the communications path.

Manufacturers have recognized this and several alternatives are available. Wireless transmission comes in the form of cellular or radio. Neither are widely used mostly due to the extra expense and difficulty of setting them up. Although cellular would seem the perfect choice in fact it is the most difficult due to the ever changing cell network. The switch from analog to digital left many alarm cellular transmitters in the dust. The industry is just now catching up but the point remains that a fixed cellular antenna is often not the best solution for a perfect signal. After all, you can move around when talking on your cell to get a better signal - the alarm system can't. However, if the cell signal can get through it does represent an extra layer of security since the typical burglar can't easily defeat it by cutting the line. We predict that cellular and internet communications will be the predominant means of alarm communication going forward.

Radio is a viable option but requires a private radio network. Some companies have tried to get around this by using other customers as 'repeaters' (which relay your signal along down the network) but this never caught on because of poor market penetration.

The vast majority of alarms use standard phone lines and if they are cut the alarm simply won't be effective except as a local alarm which will simply trigger the siren or bell. All alarm systems using phone lines do test them by sending an automatic signal to the central monitoring station- but only once every 24 hours. Then, of course, the monitoring company has to do something if the test signal does not arrive.

The alarm system can also protect itself against someone calling and trying to keep the line busy- the system will constantly hang up to keep the line clear- and it can do it must faster than one can call it. Also, many systems have two phone lines- the second for backup.

The best way to protect against phone line tampering is to simply make it impossible or difficult to cut. All telephone lines should enter underground and never be exposed. Don't assume this is impossible just because you don't have underground lines presently - the phone company will bury them- at your expense of course - in many areas.

If underground lines just can't be done, then the lines need to be installed inside metal conduit and the terminal connections inside a locked and secured metal box. This box can be tampered so that the alarm triggers if the box is opened. Effectively protecting the telephone lines is the most important thing to prevent defeat of the alarm system. Of course, looking at this the other way - it can also provide a method for your character to defeat the alarm before they break in.

Other than cutting off the alarm control panel's communications path, the industry itself has worried about the possibility of thieves 'substituting' their own control panel to mimic the target's alarm. This actually occurred a few times in the seventies, but that was when alarm controls were very crude- before the microprocessor.

Today, ultra high security Underwriter's Laboratories Grade AA rated alarms communicate via encrypted signals making substitution nearly impossible, assuming the burglar could get their hands on one to begin with. But Underwriter's Laboratories does consider the possibility, which goes like this: the thieves find out what kind of alarm control their target has and then go out and find another location with the exact same panel, which they then steal. The stolen panel is reprogrammed to the same address and 'identity' as the target panel. The stolen panel replaces the target panel but since no detection devices are connected to it, the thieves have free reign of the target.

To counteract this threat, high security alarm control panels have built in initialization codes. When the panel's memory is erased to reprogram it and it communicates with the monitoring receiver the first time, the central monitoring station receiver recognizes this as a brand new panel it has never seen before and alerts the operators with a warning message 'New Panel On Line'.

By the way, a little known fact is that Underwriter's Laboratories (UL) rates alarms and security system, as well as the alarm company and monitoring station, for high risk / high value locations with big insurance policies. UL specifies exactly what type of alarm system a jewelry store for example, will require to even obtain insurance.

Luckily burglars are lazy so most normal business and residential locations don't have to worry about this.

The Keypad

The keypad is essentially a human interface device allowing the user, (and service technician) to interact with the system and program it. The higher end keypads all have displays that provide information to the user. Alpha-numeric displays are much preferred over simple LED lights, and are more than worth the extra money. Besides just making it easier to arm or disarm the system, these keypads display the exact 'zone' or detection device status, previous history, and diagnostics. They are also generally used for programming the alarm system by the alarm company technicians.

One program item is the entry / exit delay time. Since the keypad should always be located within the protected area, a method is needed to allow the user to get in and disarm it before the alarm trips. This is called the entry delay and is simply a time period in seconds while the system waits for a disarm code to be entered. The sequence goes like this: the user opens a door and the system detects the door opening and begins a countdown timer (usually 30- 60 seconds). If the system is disarmed within the time period no alarm occurs. If no code (or the wrong code) is entered, the control panel then transmits an alarm signal - and likely sounds some audible device like a siren.

One huge potential avenue to explore in defeating an alarm system is this entry delay. People being people, they tend to want the entry delay programmed very long. Obviously if this delay is set as long as three to five minutes, it gives a potential burglar a long time inside before the alarm goes off.

The way entry delay works is that the first time a delay door opens (each zone or device can be programmed as either delay or instant), the countdown starts. The alarm control waits the amount of entry delay before generating an alarm. Any additional devices tripped during that time period, such as motion detectors, are also ignored (as long as they are programmed as delay devices) until the alarm is either disarmed or the time delay runs out. It doesn't matter if the door is closed behind you or not, once the cycle starts it cannot be stopped unless the system is disarmed.

The exit delay is the opposite and allows the user time to arm the system and then walk through the door. As long as the door is closed within the allotted time the system is then armed and no alarm occurs. While this method is quite effective, especially in small systems, it is not foolproof. The keypad should always be located at the door users enter and leave through.

The important point is to keep the entry and exit delays as short as possible while still allowing enough time to enter and leave. While 30-45 seconds may seem short, it is actually quite long- as long as the keypad is located correctly. At least one keypad must be located near the door employees or owners actually use to enter the building- not necessarily the front entrance. The keypad must never be placed where it can be observed from outside - burglars could use a telescope to easily discover the code (authors - paying attention?).

We also must mention that with modern keypads it is not really possible to disarm the system by taking it apart and touching wires together - that's another Hollywood myth. The keypad uses data to communicate with the control panel - shorting wires together will only damage the keypad and render it useless, but the alarm itself will still function just fine.

While electrically speaking the keypad is pretty secure, it does have inherent weaknesses from human nature. Although most alarm systems can store hundreds of PINs (allowing audit trails of exactly who armed or disarmed the alarm) many owners end up only using one PIN for everyone. This makes it much easier for a bad guy to obtain the PIN if a disgruntled employee leaves since the owner or manager will usually fail to change the PIN since everyone uses it.

Another weakness with one PIN for many users is that the numbers on the keypad can actually be worn from constant use, making it possible to narrow down the PIN. Since most people only use 4 digit pins (and like combinations with lower numbers first) it may be possible to guess the PIN by the wear on the keypad.

And of course, as we said, , there is always the possibility of simply observing a user entering their PIN. If the keypad is located in a highly visible area, it may be possible to observe it- whether from outside, by remote camera or telescope, or even by following a person in on some pretext. Keypads should never be located opposite windows or glass doors for this reason and avoid placing them in public areas at all if possible.

EOL (End of Line) Supervision

Just a word on 'supervision' - this is a term used to describe how an intrusion panel insures that all the wiring in a security system is intact. Supervision makes sure that no wires are cut when the system is disarmed or armed. A resistor of a specific value- usually 1000 ohms or 3000 ohms- is placed across the circuit at each detection device then the control panel sends a constant voltage through this circuit and measures it. If the voltage drops or the current increases, the panel senses the change as either a short or open and alerts the user or transmits a trouble signal. This configuration also prevents some burglar from shorting wires together to bypass an alarm door – like you see in the movies.

The Sounder

Although almost all systems have some sort of sounding device like a bell or more commonly a siren, they are really of little benefit except to warn the burglar he has tripped the alarm.

We tend to favor extremely loud, penetrating sirens which serve mostly to un-nerve the burglar and hurt his ears. There are peizo type sounders which can be so piercing that the average person can't stand to be in the area for more than a few minutes. This is a real nightmare for burglars and may save valuable property by chasing the burglar away while the police respond.

Unfortunately, many alarm system owners get upset at the sounder being too loud so they tend to want something low key- until they actually experience a break-in.

All sounders are generally supervised, by the way. Cutting wires to sounders will only serve to transmit an alarm to the central monitoring station and warn the police even earlier.

Contacts

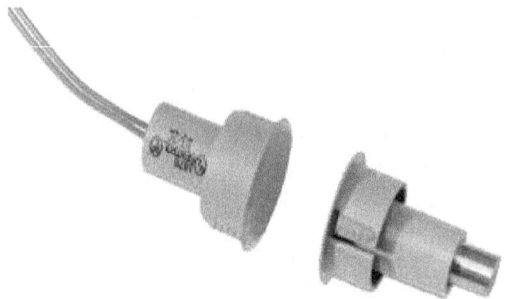

Concealed type of Door Contact

The door contact consists of two parts- a magnet and a switch. The magnet is installed into a hole bored in the door itself (the swinging part). The switch is installed in the frame (the fixed part) since the frame doesn't move the wires are run from the switch to the alarm control panel. A big feature of the hidden or concealed contact is that the wires are by design also concealed or hidden- making it nearly impossible to attempt to bypass the contact by interfering with the wiring.

Older systems and cases where the door is set in solid concrete often use surface mount contacts. The big flaw here is that the wires (and the switch) are exposed to tampering.

A typical surface door contact

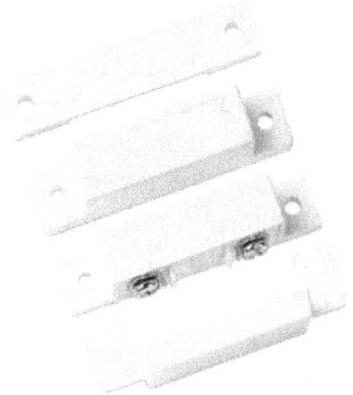

Another type of surface contact where even the terminals are exposed.

The bottom part is a cover that is designed to protect the terminals but is rarely used. This type of contact should be avoided.

As we stated, the first line of defense is, and always has been, the door contact. We are writing about the contact first because it is a key component of 'perimeter detection'.

Nearly 99% of the time, the contact consists of a two part unit- a magnet and a reed switch. The magnet goes on the moveable door and the switch is mounted on (or in) the door frame (which doesn't move). The wires are connected to the switch, while the magnetic doesn't require any connection so it's free to move open and closed.

When the door is closed, the magnet is brought up next to the switch and its magnetism holds the reed switch closed, completing a circuit. Almost all burglar alarms depend on this closed circuit principal, this is so if a burglar attempts to cut any wires anywhere while the system is armed, it will trip and transmit an alarm signal. The control panel also monitors this wiring while the system is off or disarmed by the way. If a wire is open when you go to arm the system, the control panel will warn you.

Once the system is armed, any opening of the door either by key or by force, will trip the alarm. It is important to note that the alarm cannot detect whether the door is locked or unlocked- only if it is open or closed. Many customers mistake this. Sometimes they forget to lock their door and when they return realize it was unlocked all night and blame the alarm company. If the alarm company did not receive any alarm signals over night, it means no one actually opened the door- even though it was unlocked, (consequently, a lucky occasion for the owner).

Most door contacts are fairly sensitive and if the door is opened more than an inch or so, it will set off the alarm. There is somewhat of a fine line here - the contact must be sensitive enough that the door cannot be opened too far, but forgiving enough not to alarm on wind and rattles.

Garage doors, roll up doors, and overhead doors all function the same way. Large garage doors use larger and sturdier magnets and switches.

Since alarm contacts are by their very nature magnetic, they have an inherent weakness in this regard. The typical basic alarm contact cannot differentiate between 'its' magnet and a foreign magnet. If the switch is the exposed surface variety, it is possible to bypass the contact with another magnet. We have seen many instances of this in warehouses and distribution centers where employees tape their own magnet to the alarm contact so they can open the door during the day without setting off alarms. Of course, this requires access to the alarm contact from *inside* the building.

It is also possible to slip some magnetic material through the door frame from outside the building in the vicinity of the contact and bypass it. Thin magnetic material such as used in refrigerator magnets will sometimes do the trick- assuming the gap between the door and the frame is wide enough to insert it.

This is extremely tricky since you have to insert the magnetic in exactly the right place and hold the magnet strip in place while forcing or jimmying the door. Even if you succeed that far, you must continue to hold the magnet while opening the door and then secure it while inside to prevent it from falling off and tripping the alarm anyway. Very strong 'rare earth magnets' capable of activating the reed switch through three inches of wood would also circumvent the contact. Doors made of steel have a significant advantage in preventing this.

Even if you are able to insert a foreign magnet, you are not always safe. Contacts come in many sizes and configurations for specialized applications. One special type is the 'balanced' or high security contact. These have a special magnet that is matched to the switch. Once in place, if any other magnet is brought close to the contact, it will sense the wrong magnet and send an alarm. These are especially useful where the contact is subject to tampering- such in a warehouse with remote fire exit doors. It can prevent dishonest employees from bypassing the switch and opening the door to place stolen merchandise outside for later pickup.

While these types of contacts are not common, they are used on high-risk, high security applications- the very kind of place it would be worthwhile to break into.

Of course, there is still the possibility of encountering a place using surface mount alarm contacts where the wires are exposed. It is true that alarm contacts can be bypassed by shorting these wires since most contact set off the alarm by 'opening' the circuit. Be aware however, that EOL resistors are typically used to supervise such contacts and any attempt to short the contact will cause an alarm.

Motion Detectors

PIR

The next most common detection device is the motion detector, and the most widely used motion detector by a wide margin is the PIR or Passive Infrared. Over the years many other technologies have come and gone, (ultrasonic and microwave to name two), but the PIR has maintained its place as the most common motion detector.

The reasons are simple: they are relatively inexpensive (for the area coverage) and they are extremely effective and they look pretty good. Most PIRs do a good job of blending into the room's environment or décor because they are usually sleek, relatively small and unobtrusive.

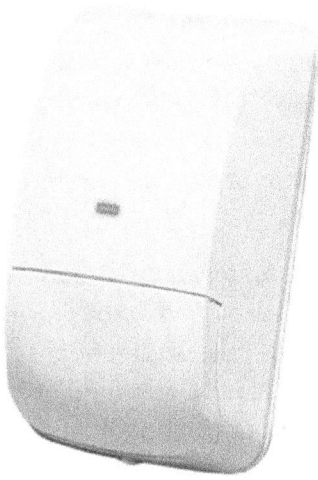

Wall Mount PIR

The walk test LED is in the middle

As its name implies the PIR is a passive device. It does not emit any beam; it simply 'looks' at an area and senses temperature changes. Think of it as an extremely sensitive and intelligent thermometer. Imagine a room at an ambient temperature of 78 degrees Fahrenheit, the PIR senses and remembers this temperature. If a foreign object enters the room in the field of view or the detection area of the PIR's sensor, the temperature will change. The PIR is very sensitive and even a change as small as tenths of a degree will be detected.

Of course if the PIR was just pointed at a room it would be alarming constantly from normal variations in temperature. Since infrared is in fact a wavelength, optics can be utilized to 'focus' the infrared energy onto the sensor. Most PIRs employ mirrors to divide the room or area to be monitored into 4 or more zones. The PIR is then programmed to look at a temperature change between these zones. If all four zones remain equal - as in a change in room temperature from heaters, then no alarm is generated.

However if a rapid change is detected between zone 1 and zone 2 then the PIR assumes an intruder has entered the area and signals an alarm. This is the reason PIRs are more effective at detecting intruder moving *across* their field of view. If the PIR is incorrectly installed so the intruder only moves towards it, then is less likely an alarm will be generated because it will not sense the temperature change between two or more zones.

Unfortunately, pets and birds also move readily across rooms and are known to generate false alarms. Pets are handled by limiting the downward detection zones to about three feet off the floor depending on the pets encountered. There is no solution for birds except to limit the PIR's use to areas without the possibility of flying birds.

Since the PIR is at heart an optical device, it is possible to set some off with an extremely bright light (such as headlights). We have also been suspicious in the past of high false alarm activity prior to burglaries - suspecting that burglars purposely tripped the PIR alarm with bright lights to lull police into slow response and then commit a burglary. This was even demonstrated on a television show which has since gone off the air. More expensive PIRs have circuitry to prevent this, but such lights can be suspect when investigating causes of false alarms.

PIRs do have a unique weakness, which is both an advantage, and a potential flaw. Infrared energy does not penetrate glass. It is not recommended to ever mount a PIR actually looking directly at glass for other reasons- namely the bright lights that can interfere with the optics - but PIRs will not sense a temperature change outside through glass.

PIRs have few inherent weaknesses. One is a detection gap under the detector because it can't 'look' straight down. It is possible to exploit this weakness if the PIR is improperly installed- such as on a side wall too close to a window or door. The PIR should always be installed in a corner so crawling underneath it –from a door or window- for any distance is difficult.

PIRs also have a 'pet option' which adjusts the optics so the detection pattern is about two- three feet off the floor so pets can move around freely and not cause false alarms. This is a real weakness. If the homeowner has pets it is very likely a burglar could crawl all around the home without being detected as long as they stay very low.

Ceiling mount PIRs are popular because they can cover large areas without being blocked by furniture or equipment. They also have a gap in coverage if installed too high. Most PIRs are completely ineffective if the ceiling height is over 12 feet. At a height of 8 feet however they are killer good- except if the owner has pets of course, then the same problem applies.

Short of crawling around on the floor, which is a not a guarantee of success, there is only one real way to defeat a good quality PIR. A popular television show Myth Busters devoted several episodes to defeating alarm systems. Using an infrared camera to check their work they attempted several methods to circumvent a PIR.

First, the room was warmed to 98 degrees to offset the PIR's sensitivity. The result when a person entered was still an immediate alarm. The fact is, a PIR is much more sensitive than it needs to be. It can easily measure temperature in hundredths of a degree.

The next approach was to cool a person down. One of the crew members was dressed in a 'wet suit' and then chilled down with a CO2 fire extinguisher. Although the infrared camera showed almost no heat signature the PIR was still able to pull him out of the background and trip the alarm.

Next the person was encased completely in cool, wet mud - the PIR still tripped. No matter how slow or how fast, or from what direction - the PIR always detected the intruder. They finally found the only way to defeat the PIR was to place a sheet of glass in front of it. Remember - infrared energy doesn't penetrate glass!

Carrying around a large sheet of glass is not very practical of course, but it does raise an issue. If some other coating (such as clear lacquer (including some hair sprays) was applied to PIR it could be masked—the invisible clear layer of lacquer prevents the PIR from sensing a temperature change. This would still require the burglar have prior inside access to the PIR in order to defeat it - but it is a good potential plot device!

Ultrasonic & Microwave

While these two technologies are never used anymore, it is possible they are still installed in older locations. Ultrasonic works by sound waves transmitted and received back. If the sound waves don't return in a precise time, the detector assumes there is intruder and trips the alarm. Ultrasonic can easily be defeated, since ultrasonic is essentially just sound waves it be deflected by most materials- even a bed sheet.

Microwaves pass through walls too easily and were a major source of false alarms. Some alarm manufacturers have attempted to get around this by combining microwave and infrared into so called 'dual technology' detectors. Unfortunately, what ends up happening is you get the worst of both. The microwave stays in alarm all the time and the system falls back only on the infrared. Dual technology detectors end up just being expensive PIRs.

Beams

Beams are the active counterparts of passive infrareds (PIRs). Since these are active infrareds, they require two parts: a transmitter and a receiver. The transmitters only require power and sends an invisible *modulated* (or encrypted) infrared beam to a receiver. The receiver, once powered up, expects to 'see' the modulated infrared energy. If the receiver does not see the beam for any reason, it signals an alarm to the control panel.

Beams come in many configurations, they can vary from single beams for up to a 100 foot line, to double and quad sets which can go as far as 1000 feet. A characteristic of infrared beams is their black (really very dark red) housing and lenses. Since infrared easily penetrates even very, very dark red, the observer (or thief) cannot determine which way the beams are pointing. This is especially useful when there are multiple sets of beams converging. Active beams can be used outdoors with no problem - except as we'll discuss next.

Outdoor Beams with their distinctive black housings

Drawbacks of beams are exactly what you might imagine, when used outdoors they are prone to alarms from animals, blowing debris, and very heavy rain or snow. Indoors it can be difficult to maintain a clear path, especially if the beams are far apart. Beams do remain a very viable option to cover long distances, but when used outdoors they are often used in conjunction with cameras to allow responders or security to observe the areas when an alarm occurs.

Beams represent our all time favorite movie myth. We must have seen fifty films where the burglars put on some special headgear or goggles and are then magically able to 'see' the red beams crisscrossing some protected high value area. Sorry guys, no such goggles exist. Active infrared beams are not lasers and do not emit pencil thin beams like you see in the movies. You can't hold up a mirror or replace the beam with another.

Beams are quite effective but they do have many weaknesses. There are often gaps in coverage - especially at corners where two sets of beams coincide. Even more likely there will be gaps under the beams - purposely so as to avoid false alarms by animals. Whether one can exploit these gaps depends a great deal on their agility and is similar to the gaps in indoor PIR coverage, which are technically possible but extremely difficult in real life.

Outdoor beams usually have a 'fog' cutout. If dense fog blocks the beams to a certain percentage, the beam is temporarily disabled. Intruders could take advantage of this feature if they are willing to wait for a foggy evening (or use a fog machine?).

Another approach used by intruders when trying to defeat outdoor beams is to simply cause false alarms - repeatedly and constantly until the owner ignores them or disconnects them. I would guess from experience that easily 50% of all outdoor beams are disconnected and just remain as a visual deterrent. Intruders will often just trip one and hide to see if the police respond.

Outdoor beams can be combined with digital video technology to make them more effective so don't give up on them.

Video motion can be combined with beams - so that both have to trip before generating an alarm - and therefore solve many outdoor protection problems. In this setup, a camera is dedicated to view the same area as one set of beams and its video motion grid is then set to alarm along the beam. The output of the video motion is connected to the alarm system and 'cross-zoned' with that beam. Both devices have to trip before the alarm control transmits the alarm. A great advantage of this is that the video will show exactly what caused the alarm- and can be viewed remotely by the monitoring company or event or owner. This could be a really cool scene actually in your story.

Inside beams are another matter entirely for a potential intruder. They can be very difficult to spot in the dark since they may be shooting hundreds of feet across a warehouse, but if you know where they are you can usually easily slid underneath them. Then again they are also prone to blockage from boxes, forklifts, and other material so often internal beams are also ignored or disconnected due to laziness.

Indoor beams are meant to act as 'traps' preventing burglars from 'hiding inside' until everyone leaves for the day and / or transiting wide areas should they gain entry. For these reasons it is important not to let the general public wander around where they can map out beam locations during the day. Also don't share too much of the system design with employees who may sell the information to burglars.

Glass Break Detectors

Since the earliest alarms there has been a need to deal with glass windows. For the first three quarters of the 20th century foil was pretty much the only method available. This involved gluing fragile tin foil to the window in a continuous pattern to form a closed loop. It even became somewhat of an art form depending on the installer's skill. If the glass was broken the foil broke as well and interrupted the circuit causing an alarm. Foil was extremely effective, by the way, it was very difficult to bypass and almost always worked. You will still see many examples of foil left over from bygone days but it is almost always disconnected and not in use.

Around 1985 technology finally stepped in and glass break detectors or GBDs came into use. Glass Break detectors come in two basic types - vibration (shock) and acoustic (actually 'listening' for glass breakage).

Acoustic type glass break detectors contain a microphone and actually listen for the sound of breaking glass. Since there are so many different types of glass these detectors must be capable of detecting both plate glass (which is noisy and high frequency) and tempered (which is relatively quiet and low frequency). This presents significant issues since many other common sounds fall into these frequencies such as keys, ringing phones, cleaning equipment, and many other items.

Various styles of Glass Breaks

While acoustic detectors are fairly adept at detecting breaking glass, they also are very prone to false alarms due to the issues above. Manufacturers have built in processing power to circumvent the false alarm issues - such as combining vibration or passive infrared detection. Unfortunately, the combination technologies tend to work too well and can result in no alarm when the glass is actually broken.

The most effective glass break detection is the type that attaches to the glass or frame and detects the vibration of the glass shattering rather than the sound of it breaking. These are much less prone to false alarms as well. This type is considerably more expensive to install since there must be a minimum of one per window or window frame and there is more wiring which must be concealed.

Vibration / shock type GBDs typically do not suffer as many false alarms because they are more focused. These devices employ a piezo crystal structure which generates voltage when undergo sufficient vibration. Although they don't directly detect breaking glass per se, they are very effective at detecting break ins through windows, walls, or nearly any structural part of a building.

Like anything else, vibration sensors have their own set of drawbacks, the biggest of which are limited range (the vibrations only travel short distances) and the fact they must be rigidly attached to frames or glass (which many owners do not like due to aesthetics).

In case you were wondering- cutting a perfect hole in a glass window in next to impossible- despite what you see in the movies. Most glass windows and especially glass doors and surrounding glass fronts are tempered glass- by law. Tempered glass has a tendency to shatter in thousands of pieces when any pressure is put on it and usually can only be cut on a special machine.

Sure, there's a possibility that older buildings could still have plate glass installed but we once challenged several professional glass installers to cut a circle into a plate glass window to test several glass break detectors- three tried and failed. One was able to get a large circular cut but the glass finally shattered and tripped the detectors anyway.

Pressure Sensors

So called 'pressure sensors' which can detect a burglar lifting off the glass case protecting some valuable object are very popular in the movies. In reality, we have never seen one. I suppose one could rig up something similar, but we know of no commercially available device.

There are such things as 'mats' which are designed to be placed under carpet under windows so that if a thief entered through the window, the pressure of his feet hitting the floor would trip the alarm. Mats were only used in residential and have fallen out of favor.

High value art objects are better protected with concealed contacts, beams or even digital video. Jewelry cases usually just have contacts to detect opening the rear doors, very rarely will you see any type of alarm on the glass itself but this easily accomplished with vibration type glass break detectors.

Safes & Vaults

If you happen to have a safe or vault featured in your story, there is very specialized protection available. A typical safe protection package consists of balanced safe contacts (which sense if foreign magnets are introduced near them), shock sensor, vibration detectors, audio listening devices (which alarm on the sound of drills), and heat detectors (to sense attempt to burn through the safe or vault).

In previous times, there was also a proximity detector which could sense someone just touching the safe. These capacitance alarms were very similar to the touch lamps you see sometimes. The capacitance control was adjusted or 'balanced' via an sensitivity control. After that anyone just touching the metal safe or vault would trip the alarm.

While these were very effective (when they worked) they were also prone to mis-adjustment and false alarms, the main reason being environmental. While the adjustment would be perfect for 72 degrees and 50% humidity, as soon as the room temperature or humidity changed, so would the sensitivity! Often it changed to more sensitive and anything would set it off. As a result capacitance alarms are mostly a relic of the past.

These days safes and vaults are protected by Electronic Vibration Detection (EVD) and Vaults Sound Alarm (VSA) with high security triple biased contacts backed by PIR motion detectors covering the safe or vault area. A minimum of two PIRs are used so they can back each other up. This provides a very superior, almost foolproof intrusion system.

Sophisticated safe and vault alarms are extremely effective and nearly impossible to defeat in any way despite what you might have seen. These alarms are almost always (and certainly should be) on separate areas or zones so that even if the main alarm system is disarmed or bypassed the safe or vault is still armed and active. The slightest vibration from a drill or heat from a burning bar or torch will trip these alarms long before a burglar can get the door open.

VSAs are capable of monitoring multiple microphones and can protect very large vaults. Sound detection is the perfect medium for vaults - after all, vaults are by their very nature extremely quiet environments.

This is another source of amusement to security professionals.

VSAs will pick up the tiniest sound long before a burglar could gain entry. Of course, safes and vaults have played a huge role in many movies. There has been numerous heart pounding scenes of burglars performing elaborate schemes to get inside a vault. If you think back though, you'll remember that the story line almost always involved breaking into the safe or vault - some of them quite ingenious – but not actually bypassing the alarm. By the way, my favorite was the movie where the burglar used water to fill the vault and then blew the door off from high pressure build up inside. The same cable television show tried that one too- with absolutely no success.

While this is all in good fun, people with real vaults are not usually stupid enough to leave some major weakness in their system. Safes and vaults don't exist by themselves; they are surrounded by the rest of the building which also has alarms. Every safe and vault not only has its own internal alarm, but numerous motion detectors pointing at it, not to mention all the rooms leading to it.

The biggest danger to vaults is in fact their location. If the location is old, the surrounding building may have changed considerably over the years - potentially leaving open a weakness that can be exploited.

Some examples would be nearby tenants who have vacated, leaving their adjoining space unoccupied and a haven for burglars to work all weekend to gain entry into the back of your vault. Another would be underground parking which is directly below the vault and can be used to gain entry through the vault floor.

Breaking into a vault requires heavy equipment and lots of knowledge- that's the best way to counteract such attempts. The fact that safe cracking and vault break-ins are so difficult is demonstrated by how rarely it actually happens. When is the last time you read about such a break-in in the newspapers?

Burglars are for the most part very lazy and too not bright. They favor 'smash and grab' techniques and will usually move on to targets that are not protected by alarms.

The fact of the matter is though: no matter how hard a burglar works to get into a safe or vault the extreme probability is that an internal sound detection system will have the police on their way long before they gain entry.

Wireless Alarm Systems

No discussion of intrusion alarms would be complete without mentioning wireless alarm systems. For many years manufacturers sought to alleviate the high labor portion of installing intrusion alarms with limited success. Eliminating wiring, especially in residential applications, has significant impact on the total cost of security systems. But the early wireless systems were a poor compromise at best.

Modern advances in wireless technology- especially the availability of higher frequencies in the gigahertz range- have tilted the chart towards wireless in certain applications. Unfortunately, wireless is not an ideal complete solution because wireless equipment and devices tend to be much more expensive than standard devices. There is a certain point where wireless loses any advantage over labor savings and it is usually only in rather small systems.

Wireless alarms are not generally used (nor recommended) in

commercial environments except for very specialized uses such as panic and holdup alarms. Wireless panic and holdup buttons are widely used and effective. Although the battery caveats still applies, modern wireless systems will alert the customer- and the alarm company- when batteries need replacing.

Modern 'digital' wireless systems are fairly sophisticated and nearly impossible to jam with any readily available equipment. The control panel checks in on all it's wireless devices at least once a day –and sometimes every few minutes- to make sure they are functional and reporting back. Probably the only practical way to defeat one is act on the battery weakness. Wireless PIRs draw a lot of power and can wear down batteries faster than other wireless devices. One could conceivably exploit this by tripping a PIR constantly until the battery goes at which point it will probably take at least a day to get the alarm company out to replace it leaving a window open for intrusion. Of course again you must have daytime access to the location.

The latest trend is to combine wireless alarms with cellular transmission – making for a completely 'wire free' system. Often these systems combine the control panel, the keypad, and the cellular communicator into one wall mounted unit. While this makes for a convenient, easy to install (and cheap) system it also introduces an incredible new weakness: a burglar can simply break in and before the entry delay expires, rip the unit off the wall and smash it, preventing the alarm signal from ever getting through.

Central Monitoring Stations

To be effective the alarm system must be monitored either by in house / on site security guards or by some outside party. While you could simply just sound a siren or ring a bell upon an alarm, it is pretty clear this wouldn't accomplish much unless you have neighbors that are present 24 hours a day and willing to call the police. The police themselves almost never accept alarms directly, so the only alternative is to contract with a central monitoring station. Usually, the alarm company that installs and services your alarm will monitor it. In some cases they may contract it out to a third party.

Even if there are on site security guards, the alarm system also be monitored by a central station as a backup. This serves many purposes. First, if the guard should become incapacitated or disabled, the alarm will still be handled. Secondly, if the guards should be subverted (paid off) by burglars, then the alarm monitoring company will still be there to notify the police.

In any case, the monitoring company is obviously critically important. Your security ultimately depends on their action or inaction. When an alarm is received at the central station, an operator must interpret it and take the appropriate action- such as notifying the police. Sounds simple doesn't it? The problems arise when the operator must begin to make judgment calls regarding the signals.

If a particular location is prone to causing false alarms, improperly arming or disarming, or forgetting to turn the alarm off; expect the operator to hesitate before doing anything. It's not possible for human beings to do perform the correct action every single time. If you generate a dozen false alarms and then the thirteenth one is real, you can't expect a good outcome. The operator can't read your mind and cannot know what is going on at the premises.

Central Station

What's it like in a central station? Very hectic! Consider that central stations are open and manned 24 hours a day, 365 days a year. Unlike even the phone company, central stations never close. There are no holidays, no down time. Someone always has to be on duty and usually at least two people are there at all times. A central station is very similar in operation- and stress level to an air traffic control center.

Central stations or monitoring companies range in size from small local concerns to nationwide centers with hundreds of employees. Some central stations have only one or two large customers- they may contract with a school district or local government. Some are even run by the company they monitor. For example, some large chains or even school districts run their own central station.

Before computers came into use, alarms were displayed in central stations by mechanical means- dials, meters, lights, buzzers, and even paper tapes. An average central station may have had 5000 or more alarms so operators were kept very busy running from rack to rack handling 'openings' and 'closings' as well as alarms. Typically when a customer armed his system, the display in the central station would change by lighting up and buzzing. The operator would then turn a dial putting the system into night mode and clock a time card for that customer. No one ever fell asleep in a central station!

If the dial, meter and buzzer indicated an alarm, the operator had to find the correct dial, look up in a book who the customer was and what to do and clock a card with the time. Even though a shift might have 5 or more people on duty, there were many occasions when multiple alarms had to wait for the next available operator

Today, central stations are quieter, with rooms full of computer displays. Systems are more automatic so openings and closings are handled by the computer and logged without the operator having to take action. While that may seem to take a large workload off the operators, the job is in fact tougher than ever. Monitoring companies today may handle 10,000 customers or more.

Incoming alarms, trouble signals and other monitoring points arrive on displays in order of priority and with colors indicating the type or importance of the alarm. The operator or 'customer service representative' must determine from a database of information and instructions what action to take. Usually, they will notify the police or fire department dispatch center but often the type of signal dictates other actions such as notifying the customer or a maintenance person.

Unfortunately, the vast majority of signals arriving in the central station are false alarms- as many as 99% of all alarms are false. This means the operators are busy handling false signals when the occasional actual alarm arrives. This is also the area where there is room for error.

There has been much discussion in the monitoring community about 'operator judgment calls'. Should the central station operator decide whether to notify the police or should they just do it on every alarm? Either way the monitoring company employee is put in a difficult situation. They may indeed call the police time after time on the same alarm from the same customer and endure the wrath of a police dispatcher who won't dispatch patrol cars anyway. But the very time they make a judgment call and not call the police will be the time the alarm is real.

The term central station is not used as often today because the name is confusing to the public, most prefer the term monitoring company. Also traditionally the term 'central station' was used to denote a UL Listed facility with guard response.

UL (Underwriter's Laboratories) lists and approves alarm systems for insurance companies. In order to obtain insurance, it is required for high profile targets like jewelry stores, to install a UL Listed alarm system. The highest grade system is rated AA and is usually reserved for high risk / high value targets such as jewelry stores.

Central Stations are tested and inspected once per year. A UL inspector will check each alarm record and the response time. Sometimes the inspectors would even cause an alarm with the help of a customer, and test the alarm company response. If the central station falls too far below averages, they risk losing their UL listing-, which means they could lose many, many high paying customers.

It was quite common up to the 1990's for central stations to dispatch armed guards to investigate the cause of alarm. UL in fact demanded response on certain types of burglar and fire systems in a specific time period. Certain high grade burglar alarms (Grade A) required response within 15 minutes.

Alarm company guards routinely carried keys to the customer's premises with the idea that guards and police would be able to gain entry and search the premises. Even as far back as the mid 70's police response was erratic or slow and many time the alarm company guards searched the buildings by themselves.

As populations, traffic, and liability concerns grew, armed response by central stations began to decline until today when it is very, very rare. At best, the central station or the customer will contract with a patrol service to respond. This adds considerable cost but at least it guarantees action will be taken on alarms the police will likely ignore.

Interestingly enough, we are not aware of any instances where the central station itself was attacked. UL has always recognized that possibility and has strict standards for securing the building. In fact, UL specifies the monitoring area itself should not have windows if it is on the ground floor, and doors must be locked and controlled at all times.

Attacking the monitoring company would render the alarms they monitor useless since no police would be notified of any alarms. There have been instances of evacuations due to bomb threats or hazardous spills in the neighborhood and we have always suspected these may have been caused for ulterior motives but nothing was ever proven. Today with the advent of national monitoring stations, attacking the central station is much more complicated and much less likely.

So, can alarms be defeated?

You've probably seen many a movie demonstrating how burglars defeat high tech security systems. Hollywood has perpetrated the myth that alarms can be defeated, but like most things in Hollywood, the reality is quite different.

With current technology, a well designed, maintained, and tested intrusion system is in itself almost impossible to defeat. A cable television show devoted several episodes to defeating various intrusion technologies and discovered just how difficult it was.

The key is a well designed system. All doors should be alarmed, and backed up by motion detectors. Motion detectors should be infrared sensing and must be placed at no more than eight feet high and always so that the intruder must pass across their field of detection- never facing. The alarm door contacts and the PIRs (Passive Infrared) motion detectors act as back ups to each other. There are many variations on alarm contacts to suit different installation requirements. Your alarm company will choose the right one for each application- such as overhead doors.

Should a burglar get through a wall or window, the PIR will detect them and vice versa. PIRs generally have an effective range of 40-50 feet. While there are models that have longer range, we recommend staying away from them due to issues with false alarms. It is simply very difficult to control the environment hundreds of feet away from the detector.

PIRs should never face glass. Although infrared does not pass through glass- the intense light from the sun or headlights can cause the sensor to alarm. Glass is in fact the PIR's only weakness; don't expect a PIR to detect motion on the other side of internal office windows or showroom display windows. And it is true that if a burglar could somehow place a sheet of glass in front of a PIR it would no longer detect motion, that just isn't too likely.

The best defense to avoiding any problems with PIRs is just to test them. All PIRs have a 'walk test light', an LED on front that lights up when it senses motion. Make it a point to walk in front of your PIRs periodically and ensure the LED is coming on. This will also alert you if somehow the power is cut to the unit - although the PIR should be powered from the alarm control panel - and *it* should detect any problems with power immediately. Of course burglars can use this feature by casing the place during the day and determining range and blind spots of motion detectors.

Longer distances such as hallways or warehouses can be protected with active infrared beams (also know as PECs – Photo Electric Cells a holdover term from the older days). Although some people refer to these as 'lasers' they are not. These consist of a modulated transmitter and receiver pointed at each other. As the television show so rightly proved, these cannot be seen with powder or special goggles - despite what you've seen in movies. They are completely invisible and it is impossible to use a mirror to reflect the beam back on itself. One reason is that no one knows which side is the transmitter since both transmitter and receiver appear identical.

Glass break sensors are very popular but we only recommend them as a last resort and never, ever as primary protection- only as a backup. The really effective glass breaks are based on vibration or piezo effect and are mounted to window frames or glued directly onto the glass.

All other glass breaks are acoustic, these actually listen for the sound of breaking glass. These are generally either a false alarm nightmare or fail to detect breakage at all. Even worse, the latest trend is to combine a PIR and an acoustic microphone in the same detector so that if the PIR senses motion, the glass break is disabled. This is supposed to eliminate false alarms from janitors or employees, but it more likely to result in no alarm during a real burglary.

Alarm companies no longer install ultrasonic or microwave type detectors or 'dual technology' sensors. Ultrasonic can easily be defeated, (ultrasonic waves can be deflected by a bed sheet), and are almost never used any more. Microwaves pass through walls too easily and are a major source of false alarms. Some alarm manufacturers have attempted to get around this by combining microwave and infrared into so called 'dual technology' detectors. Unfortunately, what ends up happening is you get the worst of both. The microwave stays in alarm all the time and the system falls back only on the infrared. Dual technology detectors end up just being expensive PIRs

There are some serious considerations with the alarm control panel and communication. All alarm panels must communicate with the outside world in some manner to transmit an intrusion signal. This is one of the major weaknesses of most alarm systems. Traditionally, the alarm transmission is over voice grade telephone lines. The alarm panel actually dials the phone number of the central monitoring station and transmits an encoded data stream. Once the central monitoring station receives the alarm, their computers automatically bring up your account in the database and they then notify the police.

Obviously, if the phone line is cut then the alarm signal will not go through. For this reason, it is extremely important that the phone line be protected or hidden. The larger the facility the less the chance of burglars cutting phone lines because there are so many. There have been instances however, when thieves cut ALL the lines entering a building (and even an entire industrial park) to make certain they disabled the alarm they were targeting.

In any case, phone lines for alarms should never be marked or identified with tags. They should be in conduit from the point of entry to the alarm control. This can be very difficult when lines are fed from overhead poles since the phone company is just going to drop the line down the side and into the building leaving them exposed.

An alternative to dial up alarm transmission is that internet monitoring we spoke about. The alarm uses a broadband internet connection such as DSL or a cable modem to contact the central station. The big advantage of this scheme is that is can be two way. The central station's computers can be programmed to automatically and periodically contact the alarm panel to make sure it is there. Of course these internet connections generally use regular telephone lines too but at least if the line is cut or disabled, the central station can detect this in as little as 90 seconds.

Some very high risk businesses such as jewelry stores are usually required by their insurance companies to have a UL Listed alarm system. Depending on the UL Listing, they will likely require this two way form of communication. This is often referred to as 'Line Security'.

The consideration in all cases must be however, what to do if the line is disrupted? The central station gets a trouble message indicating communication was lost with the alarm control panel. UL usually requires a police dispatch, but in reality the police would not even know what to look for, if there was no outward evidence of a burglary they would simply chalk it up to another false alarm and move on to the next call.

The owner would be notified, but is there really anything they could do or would want to do? If you are concerned about this, the only real solution is to subscribe to some sort of alarm response patrol service. Many alarm companies and some guard companies will provide an armed response. Although it can be somewhat costly, it could be worth it for high risk targets who will never have to worry about police response.

So assuming that there is good alarm detection equipment and good alarm communication, can the alarm system be defeated? Human error becomes the single biggest weakness- as in most things.

There is room for human error on the part of the alarm monitoring company. If the alarm company operators are overwhelmed with too many variations of schedules and special instructions it becomes easier for them to misinterpret a situation.

An interesting twist for high risk locations is to have the system programmed with 'Duress codes'. This is a special unique PIN combination that differs from your normal arm/ disarm code. If you are under duress and forced to disarm your system by thieves, using the special duress code disarms the system as usual but also sends a special message to the central station indicating you are being forced to open your business or home.

This brings us back to the major weakness of alarm systems - human error. If the employees, or family constantly (or even occasionally) cause false alarms, the system is as good as worthless. Police departments not only keep records of false alarms (usually for fines) but the patrolmen are very aware of them. If they recognize the location as having had false alarms in the past, they are not going to get there with any particular speed and probably not at all. On the opposite side, if there has never been a false alarm at the location, the police are much more likely to respond quickly.

We have also seen numerous instances of repeated false alarms leading up to actual burglaries. Professional burglaries have been known to cause alarm after alarm until the police grow tired of responding, then they can break in at their leisure with the knowledge they have extra time inside.

Causing false alarms can be done in various ways on poorly designed systems: shining powerful spotlights on PIRs pointed towards windows, rattling windows until acoustic glass break detectors go into alarm, shaking loose doors, etc. The best way to combat this problem is to make sure none of these problems exist and to demand immediate service of any false alarms. One false alarm is cause for serious concern, but once any false alarms occur it can be months before that memory fades from the alarm monitoring company and the police department.

Many police departments are now demanding 'alarm verification' before they will even respond. Such verification usually consists of audio from the premises indicating a burglary is taking place. This was pioneered by Sonitrol and is quite effective, except that it is also very expensive since the monitoring company operators can handle less traffic because it is time consuming to listen-in on each alarm signal received to weed out the false ones.

A promising new technology avoids some of these issues and guarantees verification by sending pictures taken by motion equipped cameras to the central monitoring station along with the alarm. Which still in its infancy, this would seem an extremely effective alarm detection and deterrent system.

There are also ways to defeat an alarm if one has physical access to the system. It is possible for an expert to bypass detection devices and then return after the system is armed and gain entry- assuming the owner did not test the system before leaving. It is also possible that an inside person, such as a security guard, acts to aid accomplices to defeat the system from within. An alarm could also be defeated by disabling communications to the monitoring center – as long as there is no line security in place to detect this.

Intrusion systems that are backed by armed guard response and monitored by diligent professionals are extremely difficult if not impossible to circumvent. This is why you rarely hear of a large burglary of expensive items. When you do, it is very likely an inside job where the system was bypassed from within by 'authorized' personnel.

So while the hardware of a modern well designed security system is frankly almost impenetrable, it is the chain that still has weak links: Humans - Communication – Response.

Humans are inherently lazy so they only use one code to the system and that is easily compromised.

Humans continually set the alarm off and false alarms pile up, contributing to slow or no police response.

The phone line is cut so no alarm ever gets through.

The police are too busy so they never show up hence negating any deterrent value of the alarm.

The burglar just ignores the alarm and does the smash & grab and never gets caught.

For the alarm to do its job it must be armed, it must transmit the alarm signal, the signal must get through, the monitoring company operator must respond and notify the police, and finally the police must actually respond and show up. Just remember that humans are their own worst enemy and the weakest component of any security system.

Okay so now that we've bored you with all the technical details - how can my character defeat the alarm system?

First we need to determine the time period your story is set in. If it's pre-1990's then you have a whole set of problems: alarms were less sophisticated, but communications were more sensitive, more humans were involved, and police response was much better. From the 1950's all the way to the late 80's there was literally a pair of dedicated wires running directly from the alarm system premises to the Central Monitoring Station with lot's of live real people watching. Any break in those wires (windows breakage, door opening or an attempt to cut those wires) was instantly brought to the attention of the alarm operator via a mechanical meter, who would then notify the police, usually via direct hot line to dispatch.

A typical central station in 1980. Each dial represents one alarm.

One method is to insert a very thin strip of magnetized metal between the door and frame where the alarm contact is mounted. This would hold the alarm contact closed while the door is opened and the burglar slips in.

Another possible scenario is if the character has access to the premises they want to break into during the day. These early systems were prone to jumping out and bypassing alarm contacts. The burglar could go into the business while it was open and surreptitiously place a wire jumper across a back door alarm contact and then return later and break in through that bypassed door.

It is also technically possible to bypass the control panel at the communication line with a resistor, but this would cause a disturbance which would signal the alarm company operator. Your only hope would they that they would ignore it. But keep in mind these people were extremely conscientious. They were part of the local community. They lived to catch burglars and would never hesitate to call the police - with whom they were usually on a first name basis.

Your best bet with a pre-90's alarm system would be either: generate a rash of false alarms by shaking the door, thereby causing the police to slow down their second or third response and eventually ignore it altogether, or create a disturbance in the area which would draw off police resources while your character burglarized his or her target.

Interestingly enough weather was also a huge factor back in these days. A thunderstorm would typically generate hundreds of false alarms as the front moved through the city. Each flash of lightning would bleed over into telephone lines and cause surges which would trigger alarms. We fondly recall being in the central station and watching the path of a storm by the numbers of alarms going off.

From the 1980's through the 1990's alarm systems were in transition. Communication costs were rising so the digital dialer we discussed earlier were coming into play. These digital dialer systems were prone to telephone line cutting, which would not be detected by the alarm company for up to 24 hours - an opening for your burglar as long as they dealt with the alarm bell or siren.

Keep in mind these systems were never used on high value targets like banks, jewelry stores, precious metal facilities, or furriers. Those types of businesses were required by insurance to have UL Grade AA systems which would signal a communications line break within six minutes. Your option in this case would be to depend on that six minute window - plus the time for the alarm operator to check and notify the owner and then the police - plus the police response time (which was starting to get longer and longer by the mid 90's). So your burglar could cut the line and have as much as

15-20 minutes before police or security arrived.

In the past twenty years the alarm industry underwent a radical change. Digital dialers are the norm with some cell transmissions thrown in and also 'Internet' monitoring. But the biggest difference is in the structure of the system outside the protected premise: alarm monitoring is all computerized and alarm companies have merged and are no longer local. An alarm in Los Angeles is likely to be monitored in Denver or Dallas, or New Jersey. The alarm signals are anonymous to the alarm operators, who are hesitant to call the overwhelmed police because of all the false alarms. Police response is anywhere from 20 minutes to nonexistent. All this is an opening for your character.

Of course though, high value targets will always protect themselves. Most will have off site guards or private armed alarm response who will notify the police if they find something amiss. If you want to have fun with this you can always grant your character access to the alarm system during business hours. As we said previously, all alarm are prone to internal weaknesses. The easiest would be for the potential burglar to spray the Infrared motion detectors with clear paint and then break in through the roof later.

But security in this decade now includes cameras...

CCTV

Closed Circuit TV cameras are so commonplace these days we won't bore you with too much technical detail. One thing we must cover though is their timeline. CCTV was available and used (though at tremendously high cost) as far back as the 1970's.

An interesting fact is that banks were only a relatively recent adopter of CCTV. Prior to about 2000, banks relied on hold up cameras that used film! This was because the film presented a much higher resolution picture the FBI favored for identification purposes. When a hold up took place a teller would push a hold up button which simultaneously triggered an alarm and the film camera or cameras if there were multiple exits. The camera would then run and take continuous still frames until the film ran out. When the FBI arrived they would remove the film cartridge and actually develop it in a darkroom.

As CCTV cameras slowly developed higher resolution (it still wasn't as good as film until about 2005) they gradually replaced film and more were installed throughout the bank. Since CCTV cameras were recorded onto DVRs they ran continuously and no special button had to be pushed to activate them. And there are now two types of CCTV cameras: analog and digital or IP network. Most cameras being deployed presently for security are IP addressed networked.

The term digital really means an IP based camera which streams the video over Ethernet- similar to a web cam. Analog cameras use coax cable (RG-59) which must be home run from the camera to the recording device and / or monitor. Analog cameras are solid state and use CCD sensors similar to consumer camcorders and digital still cameras, but are considered analog because of the transmission medium.

Oh yeah - that scene where the Mission Impossible guys insert a premade video loop into the CCTV feed so the guards only see a empty room? Yep, that's actually possible! You've probably seen quite a few movies in which the bad guys 'insert' a pre-recorded empty scene into the video security system while they then walk unseen in front of the cameras. There are two variations on this myth- one involves hanging a still picture in front of the camera and the other inserting a recording into the video stream.

Now the hanging still picture trick is not going to work because of focusing issues- something that close to the camera lens will be completely blurred out- CCTV cameras do not currently have auto-focus capabilities. But 'inserting' a video recording does have possibilities; of all the Hollywood myths and tricks, this one is actually technically feasible, but only under exactly the right conditions.

If a facility has a human security force, they are not watching recorded video – there would be no reason to do so. The security force will be viewing live video at all times so inserting a pre-recorded blank scene will be noticed - whether they take any action on it or not is a question. On an analog video system with coax cable you would have to insert the video signal at a point where a connector is available (such as the camera itself or a junction box) or else it would take too long to cut the cable, separate the shield and signal and connect into it. This is difficult since cameras are usually installed inside housing which often have tamper proof screws. Junction boxes are often equipped with tamper switches which may set off other alarms. Inserting such video can only be done on an analog video signal by the way, it will not work on the new IP network cameras

The best way to protect against attacks of this type is to in fact make sure all housings, enclosures and junction boxes are tampered and that your security force investigates all momentary camera problems by going out to the area and visually inspecting it.

The main weakness of a digital video recording system is again- cheap equipment and poor installation or design, along with human error.

We have seen numerous instances of recordings showing a suspect vehicle entering or leaving a facility but the license number couldn't be determined because the camera was too far away or the video was being recorded in too low quality. Another potential flaw is the amount of frames being recorded. Many people scrimp on cost so they don't record continuously in real time because hard disk storage is expensive. So instead the recorders only grab 'frames' at 5 or 10 frames a second (or less). If this number is too high (30 frames per second is real time) then the hard disk storage will be used up quickly. If this frame rate is too low then the hard disk storage will last much longer but it's likely the recorder will miss something.

We mentioned previously that the recorder grabs frames from as many as 16 or 32 cameras. What many people fail to understand is that the effective frame rate being recorded is a function of how many cameras are connected to the DVR. For example, if the DVR is recording at 30 frames per second but has 16 cameras then the effective record rate is only 30 / 16 or 1.875 frames per second. A lot can happen between the time the first camera and the last camera is being recorded. More expensive DVRs and NVRs can record 30 frames per second per camera so the lesson is once again- you get what you pay for.

Also of course, if the recorded video is not being viewed or played back, then all the video storage in the world is not going to enhance your security. Many people make the mistake of wanting to record everything or too much then complain it takes too much time to review it!

So what can CCTV cameras do - or more importantly: what can't they do? Well for one thing , no matter what you see on TV most video cannot be improved to the point you can make out details in a poor quality image. Yeah, you saw the CSI guy take a blurry video and zoom it up in amazing detail so you can recognize a reflection off a rear view mirror of a man's face or something... You've probably seen movies or television shows where such pixilated video was run through some magic program that cleared it up to a sharp image- another myth. Not gonna happen! CCTV is not a miracle science technology. It functions exactly the same as that point and shoot camera you have that you can't get a decent photo of your kid on. All digital cameras record pixels - and if the information isn't there, it just isn't there and there's no magic program from NASA or something that can fix it or enhance it. Now if the video was high quality in the first place a lot can be done to improve the recording. If its good it can be zoomed to a point. But there is a point - just try doing that with your point and shoot. You can't get information out of nothing. If you have a low resolution image such as 240 X 352 you are not able to increase it to 800 X 600, you'll just end up with more blobs. If you want a high resolution picture at the end, you have to start with a high resolution image at the recording. There are programs which can enhance a recording with too much contrast or too little brightness but that's about it.

There are very high quality cameras available now. The new breed is called 'mega-pixel' and these can take ultra high quality videos which can be zoomed to read a license plate - as long as the quality was recorded in the first place!

Can you hack into these IP cameras? Technically yes, it is possible. But you need a whole lot of highly sensitive information to be able to do it - like the IP addresses of each camera.

Video Motion Detection (VMD)

Video Motion Detection is a relatively new but very promising technology that is basically part of the CCTV surveillance system. As of the writing of this document, the only Video Motion Detection devices available are part of Digital Video Recorders (DVR) or Network Video Recorders (NVR). We anticipate that in the near future standalone cameras will include VMD circuits and relay outputs to interface with intrusion alarm panels. With the ongoing advances in digital storage technology and processing power, video motion detection (VMD) will become the standard type of motion detection.

Video motion works by 'memorizing' the scene (in pixels) and comparing any new pixels to what is in memory. Once the threshold of new pixels exceeds the old ones, an alarm is generated. The most superior aspect of VMD is of course, that you can actually see what caused the alarm!

Due to the terrorist threat, VMD is receiving much attention and research. VMD systems can already accomplish amazing tasks such as determining which way an object is heading, whether an object is stationary for a specific length of time, when an object is moving too fast or too slow, and it can determine objects of specific sizes. Companies have even demonstrated VMD systems which can determine an individual's characteristics such as color of clothes and even height and weight!

VMD can be configured to 'look' at specific areas of the picture and to have different sensitivity at different times of the day. Again, the bonus is the fact that by playing back the video you will have a picture of exactly what or whom caused the alarm.

What about darkness you might ask? New cameras as so sensitive they can pretty much see in the dark now. But burglars must be able to see as well, so the chances are they will be using a flashlight. In total darkness, a flashlight is like a beacon to a VMD system. We successfully demonstrated a VMD system in a museum where the cameras were focused on paintings. This presented an extremely low key detection method for the public visitors, while maintaining a very high level of security should they venture too close. A bonus was when the museum turned off the lights and tried to approach a painting - the would-be intruder was detected every single time. In turns out if a human can't see the camera still could! But when the human required more light, the VMD detected them even further in advance.

Digital video recorders are essentially computers with hard drive storage. The video signal from the camera is 'captured' and converted to digital through hardware and software, compressed to smaller file sizes, and then written onto the hard drive. Since computers are very intelligent, the DVR always knows exactly where the video is stored *by time*. This means you can instantly find any event or time instead of endlessly rewinding and fast forwarding.

Although convenience alone would dictate going digital, the biggest plus is the video quality does not degrade from recording to recording, it is always as good from the first second to the 30th day. Which brings us to another advantage- the ability to keep an entire months worth of video at your fingertips- no more putting in a different tape for each day!

DVRs also manage multiple cameras because they have built in multiplexers. This means DVRs grab frames from each camera and stores as many as 16 or 32 cameras on a single hard drive. Most DVRs are also capable of displaying the cameras in a multi-screen format as well.

Since the DVR is a computer and has intelligence it can do many more things. Video Motion Detection (VMD) is one of the most important. This one feature has many uses. First, VMD allows the DVR to record only *on motion*. There's no sense recording views that don't change- empty rooms for instance. With VMD activated, only images that change are recorded which greatly increases the amount of *time* that is stored on a given hard drive. So it becomes much easier to size your DVR hard drives to store at least 30 days worth of video. Secondly, VMD can be used to activate intrusion alarms when actual motion is detected. Third, the recording speed can be increased when motion is detected for higher quality video.

A word about video quality is probably a good idea at this point. Digital video at this writing is not quite up to par with analog VHS but it comes close if properly configured. Broadcast (or DVD) quality video is considered to be 20 frames per second (FPS) at about 720 X 480 pixels. This is also known as 4 CIF (pronounced SIF). DVRs can usually approach this but only on one camera or for shorter storage periods. The reason being is that 20 FPS at 720 X 480 requires tremendous processing power and huge file sizes.

The lower end DVRs usually state specifications that look good until you realize that the spec is for *one* camera. Additional cameras simply divide up the total processing power and storage. So if one camera can be recorded at 20 FPS at 4 CIF, four cameras will actually be recorded at 5 FPS and 1 CIF (352 X 240 pixels). There are very sophisticated DVRs that can do much higher rates but are considerably more expensive.

Another huge advantage of DVRs is their ability to be connected to networks. This has two important uses: one, it means if you have multiple buildings (or multiple areas in one large building), then cameras are connected in relatively short runs to the nearest DVR and then the DVRs are connected together via the network. This allows the user to manage and view multiple DVRs (and possibly hundreds of cameras) from one central location. Another use for the network is for the owner/ manager to be able to view any of his cameras from anywhere he has an internet connection.

Recorders (NVR- Network Video Recorder)

An NVR is usually defined to mean a computer with storage and software to record digital video directly from either IP video cameras or digital video *encoders*. In reality the line between DVRs and NVRs can be somewhat indistinct. DVRs usually contain the analog to digital converters necessary to change NTSC camera video to digital bits and then store it on the hard drive. NVRs on the other hand usually do not and expect to only receive digital video which has already been converted. NVRs are designed to reside on a network and receive digital video over that network and store it.

The actual NVR is usually just an off-the-shelf computer with large hard drive storage. A RAID (Random Access Intelligent Disk) array in the neighborhood of one terabyte (one trillion bytes) is the norm but systems can go lower or higher in storage capacity.

NVRs also usually come with a software client or application to manage the video playback and searching. A recent development is video forensics. These are software tools to analyze the video once it has been stored. This area is developing so rapidly that whatever we write will probably be obsolete by the time you read this, but such tools can already do amazing things.

Some common tasks are:

Object left too long (an object remains in the view for more than a programmed time period)

Object missing (an object has disappeared from the view)

Object going wrong way (usually a human- is traveling a different path from a programmed one.

Object too fast or too slow (moving through the view beyond programmed parameters)

Analytic video systems can even determine a person's height, weight and color of clothes and search for that person among other video sources. Facial recognition software can be integrated with NVRs to search for and identify persons in stored digital video.

Very soon it will be routine to grab a snapshot of a person of interest- such as a known terrorists, thief or passer of bad checks and alert a command center when that person enters a location anywhere with networked video cameras.

Access Control Systems

An Access system does pretty much what the name implies- it controls access to a facility (or just a room). In order to accomplish this, the systems needs to be able identify the persons attempting to gain access. The identification can be by Card, PIN combination, or Biometrics (a unique human characteristic such as a fingerprint).

Gone are the days of magnetic stripe and 'swipe' cards. These were too user intensive and inconvenient, not to mention caused excessive service issues. The security industry has pretty much switched to 'proximity' cards and many are now in the process of switching over yet again to 'Smart' cards.

The typical access control system consists of several components: locks, door position sensors (contacts), request to exit devices, card readers, door controllers, power supplies and a database (usually on a server).

In order to control access, the system will also need a means of unlocking and locking doors. This is accomplished by electrifying the door locks. Standard locking hardware can be replaced with similar appearing locksets that have an electric solenoid. Electric strikes (the area in the door frame where the lock plunger goes) can be added. Or Magnetic (Mag) locks can be installed which consist of very powerful electro magnets which can hold the door closed with up to 2000 lbs of force.

Since mag locks 'unlock' by removing power, some means must be installed to allow people to exit electronically. This is generally accomplished by a REX (Request to Exit) detector. A REX is an PIR which looks for people approaching the door from the inside and releasing the mag lock when motion is detected.

Mag locks cannot be defeated by pulling force. Most mag locks can exert 2000 lbs or more so it's likely the door frame would come down before the mag lock releases. We have seen instances however, where intruders place tape or thin spacers between the mag lock and the door frame. This can weaken the magnetic field considerably and allow intruders to return later and open the door. Of course, the burglar would have to have had prior access to the open door- and the alarm will still sound once the door is opened because no valid card was used.

Unlike an intrusion alarm system, the access control system always knows whether a door is locked or unlocked since it obviously controls this function. However, for the access system a means is also needed to indicate when the door is open or closed. The door position sensor accomplishes this, and it is identical to a door contact used for intrusion purposes.

In normal operation a person wishing to gain access presents their card to a reader and the system unlocks the door. The access system has a programmed time to keep the door unlocked to allow the person to pull the door open (this is called the Door Unlock Time). If the reader is close to the door, this time can be as short as 5 seconds, but if the reader is farther away or people tend to bring large packages through, it may need to be as long as 30 seconds. The problem is that if the time is too long, another person can come behind them and simply pull open the door before the time runs out. This is known as Tail Gating.

To avoid this, the door position sensor is used to monitor when the door opens and closes. The access system can be programmed to automatically relock the door as soon as it sees the door go open – (or closed depending on the type of locking hardware.) This cancels the unlock time period and prevents people from tail gating.

Another use of the DPS (Door position sensor) is to monitor Door Held Open or door open too long. Obviously if a door is propped open, your security and the access system is worthless. This is another programmable time in the access system. Once the system senses the door open, it starts a timer and expects the door to close within this period. If the door is still open after the time expires, the system usually generates an audible warning at the door alerting someone to close the door. If the door is still open after another period, a Door Held Open alarm is generated.

The last and certainly one of the most important functions of the DPS is Door Forced monitoring. This is equivalent to an intrusion alarm. As we mentioned previously, the access system expects to receive a card read before if unlocks the door. Makes sense right? But if the system senses the door opening without a card read then there are only two possibilities- either the door was broken into (forced open) or someone used a key instead of a card- either way a security violation- one slightly more critical than the other.

Special PIRs called REX detectors are used to unlock and bypass alarms when a person leaves a through a secured door. If REX detectors are used, they must be installed very carefully and set up properly. There have been instances where people have inserted long sticks from outside through the gap in the doors and caused the REX to unlock the door. REXs are designed to detect anything approaching the door, so they are very 'loose' and have a wide pattern. While this makes them more useful for detecting authorized people exiting, it can also result in unauthorized entrances. The best solution is to install two REXs on double doors- one over each leaf and narrow the pattern so it can't be manipulated form outside.

Although it is certainly possible to use keypads and PINs to identify users on an access system, it is rarely used. PINs are often shared among employees and pretty soon you find everyone using the same number which completely negates control and documentation.

Card readers are the current preferred method. Among the reader technologies- only proximity is recommended. If any company tries to sell you any type of swipe or insert reader- find someone else. There is no cost differential any longer. Proximity readers are sealed and have no moving parts. There is nothing to wear out and once installed and working will probably continue to work forever. In fact most manufacturers provide a lifetime warranty.

HID Proximity Card & Card Reader

Proximity readers, as the name implies, only require that the card be brought into close proximity with the reader, usually about 3 to 4 inches is the reading distance. Some readers go can much further, some are slightly less. The card does not have to be inserted or swiped, just held within the range of 3-4 inches for a brief period.

Proximity readers work by radio frequency. The card acts as an antenna, the reader is the transmitter and receiver. The card modifies the radio signal in such a way as to be uniquely identified as a number. The number is made up of bits (digital computer language). The higher the bit format of the card, the greater number of digits it can represent to the system. As of this writing, 37 bit cards are the norm - which can represent billions of numbers..

Smart cards are an attractive alternative to prox cards and from the user standpoint, function identically. Smart cards present many more options for other uses, now and in the future. Because of their intelligent read/write chip, they can be used for any cashless application such as vending, parking, dining, book stores and libraries; while still performing duty as an access control card. Smart cards can be direct printed with photo for photo ID badges. Barcodes can even be printed on them as well for other purposes. One smart card can serve many, many solutions.

What are the weaknesses of card access systems? People worry about duplicating these cards (it is extremely difficult to copy a proximity card) but the real problems lay in other areas. Once again, human error rears its ugly head. On older systems with low bit range cards like 26 bit, you'll find the facility code we talked about is often ignored through programming. This results in the distinct possibility that cards from other facilities or businesses will work in your system- and appear as a person in your database! For example, if your system it set to ignore the all important facility code and if a card number of 12345 is assigned to John Smith in your facility and someone with another 12345 card from somewhere else comes it- your system will still show John Smith as using his card! Not a happy situation for either of you.

Another all too common occurrence is for the system administrator to issue multiple cards to generic people like 'temp', 'vendors', 'contractors', and 'visitors'. We have seen as many as a hundred cards issued to 'temp' which results in a complete lack of security since any time any one of those cards is used it will show up on reports as simply TEMP. Even worse, if one or several are lost it is difficult to figure out which one or audit them on a periodic basis. All an intruder would have to do is get a hold of one of these temp cards and then have free rein of a building.

Another weakness of which you should be really aware is the Request to Exit detector or REX. As we previously explained, these are essentially PIRs in a special configuration. The problem is that since they are over the door, they are too close to the outside world and subject to defeat. A common trick is for a burglar to insert a thing metal rod or hangar from the outside through the gap in double doors and trip the REX- which then unlocks the door!

Biometric Readers

Biometrics is the science of using unique human characteristics for identification purposes. Common biometrics are fingerprints, hand geometry, and retinal patterns. The least intrusive and most reliable and well understood are fingerprints of course. Fingerprint readers are readily available and the least expensive of the three- although still about 4-5 times more than standard proximity or smart card readers.

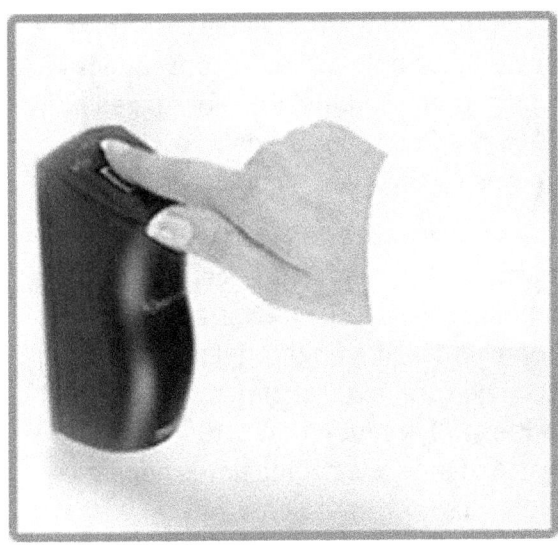

Biometric Fingerprint Reader

Although there is some psychological resistance to fingerprint readers they are still much more convenient than retinal scanning devices. Once you explain to users that the 'fingerprint' is not actually stored and can't be used by the FBI, their use is generally accepted.

Currently there are two technologies in use for fingerprint readers;

while they both use a form of optical scanning they differ in producing the actual template. The minutiae-based system is very similar to that used by law enforcement and forensics in that it records the ridges and swirls of the finger. The pattern based system can not be used for forensics since it concentrates on a 'picture' of the finger. The image is encoded and stored as a template to compare against a live finger scan. This makes the pattern based systems easier to sell to employees and unions. Once you explain that such templates can not be recovered and used for outside identification, any resistance usually disappears.

Some pattern based systems were actually originally developed for the U.S. military for smart weapons. Weapons were to have a fingerprint sensor imbedded into them with the idea that only the soldier issued the weapon would be able to fire it. Consequently, fingerprint sensors of the pattern based type are very rugged and reliable. They can scan below the first layer of skin to avoid dirt, cuts, and abrasions. Some sensors can even work under water.

So why would you want to use biometrics? PIN numbers and access cards can be swapped and shared by users, but since biometrics is tagged to an individual's unique characteristics, it is a positive means of identification. For instance, if a fingerprint is required to open a drug cabinet, you can be sure it was that person who opened it. Auditing authorities will accept biometrics without question. Many time and attendance (electronic time keeping systems) have gone to biometrics for this very reason.

Biometric readers usually require a second means of identification such as a PIN or card. The reason for this is to reduce the comparison time necessary to look up the biometric template. Understand that on a normal card reader, the only thing to be read is a number; the number is then tied to a database which contains the users personal data. On a biometric system, there is much more data. The person at the reader places his finger on the reader and that fingerprint template must be compared with the stored template. Since they could be potentially hundreds or thousands of users, there needs to be a way of narrowing down the templates to be compared. If the user is required to enter a PIN or card, the biometric already knows which stored template to compare with the live one.

One drawback of biometric readers is in fact this necessity to store the biometric template. When a new user is to be added to the system, they must be 'enrolled'. Since you can't require users to enroll at every single reader on the system, some means must be provided to download the enrolled template to all the readers. This usually requires additional wiring between each reader to distribute the templates.

Smart cards can provide a solution by writing the template to the card. When the new user enrolls, they are asked to present their smart card and the biometric reader 'writes' their template to the card itself. When the user goes to a different reader, that reader 'reads' the template from the card and compares it to the live one. This makes a very convenient system which can be deployed over multiple buildings and locations without the need for additional wiring.

Hollywood has had a lot of fun with fingerprint and retinal scanners. That popular cable television show we mentioned previously also took a crack at a fingerprint reader- and successfully defeated it! However, in this case there were almost as many holes in their methods as there was in the fingerprint reader.

First, all biometric readers have a programmable threshold of accuracy. If you set the probability of accuracy high you will get more misreads (false denials – a person that is authorized but is denied) since the system is looking for a very high standard of match before it grants access.

Conversely, if you set this threshold low, you will get very few misreads or false denials but more false positives- allowing a person that should have been denied access. Lowering this accuracy threshold could also give a burglar more of a chance to defeat the reader by using a scanned picture of someone else's finger.

Biometric readers also usually require a PIN number along with the fingerprint or other biometric before entry is granted. If you turn off this PIN feature –as apparently was done on the television show- you again make it much easier to defeat the reader. The reader being used on the show also appeared to be of lower cost and quality.

Most sophisticated biometric fingerprint readers also look for the warmth of a human finger and some even expect to detect blood pressure or pulsing as well. These make it extremely difficult to defeat them using optical gimmicks or cutting off someone's finger and using it to open a door!

Metal Detectors

Metal detectors such as commonly seen at airports are growing in popularity in schools and high security buildings. Such detectors are extremely effective and work by creating a magnetic field which is then excited by metal on a person's body, in turn creating a voltage which then sets off the alarm. This principle is based on an electrical generator. The motion of the person walking through the detector along with the metal in their pocket creates the voltage. An important point to consider is that the metal must usually be ferrous to be detected- that is, it must be able to be attracted by a magnet.

While a properly programmed metal detector set to high sensitivity is nearly impossible to defeat, one can mitigate the effects simply by walking through very slowly and not swinging your arms. I have tested this many times. If you walk through very fast, it takes a significantly less amount of metal to set off the alarm. Conversely, if you walk very slowly, you can get a significantly larger amount of metal through the detector without setting it off.

A knowledgeable operator will spot this trick and tell you to walk faster or search you manually. But in ten years of going through airports only once have we had an operator observe this.

Human error comes into play here as well. In commercial settings it is quite common to turn the sensitivity down due to false alarms. This is very dangerous since many weapons these days have little ferrous metal and could easily slip through detection.

Physical Security

Human Security Guards

The term 'guard' usually conjures up an image of an old man sleeping at his post. In fact many security guards are retired – from the military or police department. Some security guards are even off duty policemen seeking to earn extra money. It is also true they can be incompetent and lazy. Just like any other employee, there are good ones and bad ones.

It has been our experience that about 50-75% of the typical guard force is alert, competent and well trained. It does depend greatly on the company employing them too. A good guard company will provide training and roving supervisors to check on their people.

So your character or plot may encounter many types of guards. They could be seasoned professionals just out of the military engaging in part time work until something better comes along. Or a cop wanna be who actively looks for something to get involved in. Or a lazy do nothing who sleeps through his shift. Pick the one that suits your story.

Keep in mind that the lower the cost to hire the guard, the less the guard will be paid and the lower the quality of that guard will ultimately be. Don't forget, the guard company is making a profit on the difference between what the customer pays and what they pay the guard.

One big advantage of contracting out for guards is that the client pays a fixed rate. The guard company is responsible for benefits and overtime. There are reputable companies that pay their people well and provide good benefits such as health insurance and vacations. Some guard companies provide no benefits and consequently have poor employees with low morale and high turnover.

In large systems and facilities, human security personnel can be considered an essential part of the overall security system. Security supervisors should be brought in at the earliest stages to provide input and suggestions. Frequently you will be amazed at some detail or operating procedure that security is aware of that significantly impacts the overall security design.

Modern electronic security systems have several enhanced features aimed at human security. Almost any type of security signal can be directed to portable, wireless laptops, or smart phones. This includes video. Imagine a roving guard patrol, either on foot or in a vehicle, receives an intrusion alarm signal on his smart phone indicating a door intrusion on the rear of the warehouse. A video stream of the affected area is then automatically sent to his smart phone and he knows immediately if there is a problem or perhaps it's just a false alarm. Central monitoring stations often communicate with the guard force over radio for faster response.

Human security guards have many potential flaws –some of which can be counteracted and some not. Part of a good CCTV video surveillance system should always include at least one camera watching the watchers! We always recommend that guard posts, security offices, and command centers be equipped with card readers and cameras.

At the very least these will document the guards are performing their duties. If something happens, these will provide invaluable evidence of what went wrong. Lastly, these devices will also keep the guards on their best behavior since they will know they are being watched.

Such cameras and card readers should never be under the control of the guards. Partition such systems so only the management can observe, playback, or re-program such devices.

Another large threat to the guard force is bribery. Guards are usually, and unfortunately, low paid individuals which open them up to offers of cash from professional thieves to look the other way or provide inside information on the security systems.

Although there isn't much defense against this scheme, thankfully the person offering a potential bribe can never be entirely certain that they won't be reported when they try to offer one. The best way to keep your guards honest is to do everything possible to make sure they were honest in the first place.

Finally, high value targets will often have at least two guards on duty at all times- this way this is much less likelihood both guards can be subverted.

The Last Line of Defense

One of our favorite plot devices is the loyal and energetic employee who notices something amiss in the daily routine. The truth is the employees are often the last line of defense against loss. Long time employees have inside knowledge of a business which is invaluable at preventing loss. Loyal workers are loath to see others commit vandalism, abuse company property, or steal - and will delight in bringing some potential threat to the attention of their boss.

Automobiles and Other Vehicles

Okay, so you're asking what the heck cars and trucks are doing here? You know all about them, after all you probably own one. Well this section is not so much about cars as it is about *perception*.

A lot of writers don't seem to want to mention too many details about such things as cars, preferring that the reader 'imagine' what ever they want. But in our view such details add to the atmosphere and character's overall persona.

Car guys and girls notice vehicles in movies and books (when they're even mentioned). Think back to Hollywood movies you saw recently. Chances are about 85% the main character was driving a Prius or a Volvo. Why? Because Hollywood is liberal and they want to set the perception that character is as well. The truth is that Prius and Volvo have only a tiny little bit of the market share and most real car people view them as namby-pamby kind of sissy rides. Your average he-man (or villain) is not going to be caught dead in a Toyota Prius.

Maybe your character is down and out so he or she drives around in a beat up old truck. Or if you want to portray an up and coming character or family, why not an Audi? They come in many different models and sizes, they're upscale, cool, and not snobby like Mercedes or BMW.

A perfect car for the young and carefree female is the Audi TT sports coupe. If she's not quite so well off she could drive an older 2001-2006 TT (which all look exactly the same).

Now if your character is badass then the Dodge Charger in black with a Hemi V-8 engine is the ticket. They are heavy, mean, and vicious, with the aggressive hulk to plow through any obstacle and the power to get you anywhere fast. You can the tone of your story with the right vehicle: *'He makes a U-turn and heads south, enjoying the Charger's big V-8 hemi engine reverberating off the valley of downtown buildings.'*

Dodge Charger

Another go to segment for interesting rides are the 1968-1971 muscle cars. It goes without saying they are all V-8s and you have your choice of Mustangs, Challengers, and Camaros (or a Malibu) or the slighter rarer Pontiac GTO.

If your character is the rugged individualist then a truck is in order - a pick up truck of course. Ford F-150s have been the best seller since forever but there are Chevys and if you want mean then the late model Dodge Ram is the ticket.

Those are all common enough vehicles so let's have some fun and get a bit more exotic.

Jaguar - an exotic import within reach of the everyman (or woman).

Police cars - it's time to retire that all too ubiquitous Ford Crown Victoria. People, it hasn't even been made since 2011! Ford replaced it with a bad ass Taurus Police Interceptor in 2013 and it looks mean. Keep up with the times!

The point is vehicles are an opportunity to make your story stand out. Use some creativity. Do some research and pick vehicles that match your character's personality.

Post Apocalyptic Scenarios

While we're on the subject of vehicles (and this applies to military vehicles as well, we probably need to address the seemingly general lack of knowledge of what would happen after an apocalyptic event.

Certain popular television shows and movies would have you believe that somehow vehicles would not function at all or only ancient ones would be usable. This may be marginally true if an atom bomb went off because atomic bombs can generate an Electromagnetic Pulse (EMP) that is capable of burning out solid states circuits (such as those used in modern vehicles) and rendering them unable to run.

So if your apocalyptic event was caused by a world wide nuclear war then perhaps modern civilian vehicles manufactured after say 1990 would be useless. But earlier vehicles that did not use solid state circuitry would probably run fine. And since military vehicles are hardened against this type of radiation, they should survive intact. Some of this survivability is due to the fact that ignitions systems in diesel are much simpler because once a diesel engine is started it doesn't need electricity, because it doesn't use spark plugs.

But of course zombies are not known to be caused by nuclear war so we're not sure why all of the sudden everyone is walking. If I personally found myself in such a situation, the first thing I'd do is seek out a nice armored military vehicle like a Bradley personnel carrier or an M-1 tank and have at them.

There is the fuel situation to consider, but we would think that with most people gone, there would be enough gasoline left to power any vehicle you want for a lifetime. Gasoline does eventually go bad (though not for many years), but any auto parts store would supply additives to keep it fresh and usable.

And most military vehicles run on diesel fuel which can be kept stable for a hundred year with additives. We really don't think the people who survived an apocalypse would be hurting for transportation.

Police Procedure

Forget what you see on TV! There are four fundamentals concerning police procedures:

1) Most crimes are NOT solved.

2) Most of the time the victim knows the perpetrator.

3) Informants are responsible for most crimes that are closed.

4) Police rely on the fact criminals are mostly stupid.

The dirty little secret that police don't want you to know is that few crimes are actually solved.

For example - 90% of all crimes in Detroit go unsolved. FBI statistics show that somewhere between 35%-40% of homicides in the U.S. go unsolved! A state by state breakdown reveals that the more rural states are more likely to catch murderers, while the more populated are much less likely. In California and New York, for instance you have only a 50-50 chance of being caught. In Detroit you are probably, certainly going to get away with it.

And property crimes? Forget it!

Let's go back to murder. The first place the cops are going to look is someone the victim knows, like a significant other, family, and friends. The spouse is always the number one suspect. If they don't roust up a suspect there, the murder is probably not going to be solved unless the murderer stupidly leaves fingerprints and is in the criminal system, or maybe the killer runs into a police car when leaving the scene.

If the homicide is high profile, then you can expect some police heat. They will be forced to actually investigate and dig deeper. But if it's gang related or drug related, forget it even then. Sure the police will collect forensic evidence like DNA but unless the killer has been arrested before, DNA is useless.

Forensic evidence is mostly only useful for convicting someone once a suspect is apprehended. Instead, police will depend on the criminal being a blabbermouth and boasting to their friends about what they did. Then hopefully an informant will hear and tip off the cops. This pretty much goes for all types of crimes.

So, no matter what crime you're writing about, think about the implications of those fundamentals:

The likelihood of being caught is 50-50 at best.

A smart criminal that keeps their mouth shut will probably never be caught.

A hit man who doesn't know their victim or never met them prior to the murder will probably never be arrested. This is how hired killers can operate for 20 - 30 years and retire peacefully. You read about them all the time.

The fact is that police are overwhelmed with drug crime and the majority of people they encounter day to day are criminals with prior arrests and either drug dealers or drug users.

While all this sounds bleak from a writer's standpoint you can use it in your plot. Maybe your would be killer should live in a small town with an especially motivated police detective...

Small rural communities have experienced somewhat of an equalizer in recent years. The Federal government has poured millions and millions into police departments. Even the tiniest PD in Bodunk, Nowhere has all the latest technology at their disposal. Departments have computers and access to the FBI lab. They have access to national databases. They have digital radio nets that interconnect with statewide authorities.

Additionally, almost all police vehicles these days have computer data terminals which can access databases. Radios are interconnected to county, state, and regional networks. Many vehicles have cameras and even license plate scanners that automatically look for stolen and wanted vehicles. The vehicle probably has a cell phone data sucker and a driver license swipe reader that can detect forged licenses. In the trunk there is probably an assault rifle or even an automatic weapon. The cop is wearing a bullet proof vest and the car itself may even be armored. The standard Police Interceptor from Ford has crash protection up to a 75 MPH rear ender and can be optioned for armored doors and windows. I'd be more afraid of the average police patrol then a savvy detective!

While we're on the subject of patrol cars, let's discuss the typical police organization:

A police department is usually loosely based on a military organization. They have ranks, but are all over the map so all you can do is pick the area your story is set and do some research for that department. Department in the East follow military ranks more faithfully while the other end of the country does not. One fact that doesn't change much is that uniformed officers and plain clothes officers have separate ranks and structures. Detectives outrank uniforms - but only up to a point - when it comes to sergeants and above things can get messy.

Police departments are organized by areas and it often depends on how the city government is structured for voting and political office.

Some cities have precincts, others districts, and in the south parishes. Patrol cars are assigned by these areas, but can cross over when needed.

There are then counties, regions, and the entire state. On top of this are the federal law enforcement units (which are so varied and plentiful they are beyond the scope of this guide).

One hotly debated topic among law enforcement (but not citizens for some unknown reason) is one-man versus two-man police cars. The reason for having only one police officer per vehicle is strictly economic. Simple logic would tell you that this policy results in half the manpower covering the same area. (Humans are much more expensive than vehicles by the way). The problem comes when the situation turns potentially violent and requires two or more officers to respond. Some departments won't dispatch a single car to an alarm or fight or domestic dispute or even a loud party, so the first car to arrive ends up waiting near the scene for a backup - further delaying response. And the one man car patrol areas tend to be spread thinner, causing a backup unit to have to rush across town. One man cars are a questionable policy from all points of view. It is interesting to note that of America's largest cities, New York and Los Angeles have always used two man cars while many surrounding communities use only one man cars.

One creative suggestion when it comes to police in your story - please, please don't make them all incredibly stupid just for the sake of a plot device. Lately we've read a few books where advancing the plot depended on the cops being dumb. In one story the villain tailed police units to a victim's hidden safe house not once, but different locations! You may get away with this once but not twice. Cops are acutely aware of their surroundings, especially patrol cops. Do you seriously think they're not going to notice a car following them for miles and miles?

And television is worse. Both "The Blacklist" and "The Following" make the FBI out to be morons. They walk blindly into traps, they never call for backup, and they're as gullible as children. Okay, he FBI ain't what they're cracked up to be, but geez they're not all stupid either. They do have successes and they do catch criminals.

Can't we just once have a story where the police outsmart the criminal, or at least outsmart him some of the time, once maybe?

Firearms

Before we get into the weapons themselves, some clarification is in order. Ammunition is of course what you put into a firearm, but as simple as that sounds, it is cause for a lot of confusion. The term 'bullet' refers only to part of the ammo - the part that kills. A better term for one piece of ammo is a 'round'.

A 'round' of ammo consists of a bullet, a shell casing , gunpowder, and a primer.

The bullet part is made of lead and in military use jacketed with copper (as mandated by the Geneva Convention.

The shell casing is made of brass and filled with gunpowder. At the back end of the shell is the primer.

The firing pin of the gun, which is a sharpened point of steel, hits the primer when the trigger is pulled and that in turn ignites the gunpowder which causes the bullet to be expended through the gun barrel.

A 'shell' can also refer to a large caliber artillery round, such as 'artillery shell'.

Speaking of caliber - it is a measurement of the diameter of the bullet. The most common calibers are .22, .25, .357, .38, .380, .44, and .45 inches .and the metric sizes 9 mm and 40 mm for handguns. .38 cal and 9 mm are roughly equivalent.

Rifle calibers range from .22, .223, .270, .30, .308 inches to 5.62 mm and 7.62 mm in metric sizes. .223 and 5.62 are equivalent, as are .308 and 7.62 mm.

Shotguns, due to their large barrel diameter use the measurement of 'gauge' - 16 gauge and 12 gauge being the most popular. 12 gauge is larger than 16 gauge.

These caliber sizes are misleading when it comes to firepower and stopping power because each round has a vastly different shell casing size. The longer the shell casing the more gunpowder it contains. For example a .44 Magnum is much more powerful than a .45 round because the .45 casing is shorter. The same goes for the .357 and .38. Likewise a .380 though the actual bullet is the same size as the .38, has much less power because the shell casing is smaller.

The same goes for .22 and .223. The .22 is tiny whereas the .223 is much larger both in length and diameter (the shell casing is necked down).

Hand Guns

Also called 'pistols'. These can be divided into two groups: revolvers and automatics. You should understand that the term 'automatic' as commonly used is technically a semi-automatic. These weapons fire one bullet each time the trigger is pulled. A true automatic fires many bullets as long as the trigger is held down and are illegal outside of law enforcement and military.

The semi-automatic has the advantage of rapid fire and capacity since they have magazines, which generally hold from 10 to 15 rounds. The problem is that they can jam at inopportune times, and they eject damning evidence, in the form of spent shell casings, all over the firing area. Because the automatic pistol is ready to fire instantly it requires a 'safety' to prevent accidental discharge.

A revolver only holds six rounds but never jams and retains the spent shells. It is also considered more accurate because the barrel is fixed and firmly attached to the frame. The revolver functions differently than an automatic: when you pull the trigger the cylinder containing the round rotates to the next available slot and then the trigger is moved back and released, and it requires much more effort to fire. Because of this revolvers do not have or need a safety.

Popular revolvers include Smith & Wesson .38 Special, Smith & Wesson .357 Magnum, Colt Python .44 Magnum, and Rugers.

Popular automatic pistols are the Glock, Berretta, Colt, S&W, Browning, Lugar, and Rugers.

The Glock in 9mm and 40mm practically own the law enforcement market. They are lighter due to a polymer frame and have a very unique built-in safety which requires no action on the part of the shooter.

So with these facts in mind it would be improper to write: "Harry flipped the safety off his Smith & Wesson .44 Magnum and pulled the trigger." - because it is a revolver and doesn't have a safety. And neither do the Glock automatics because the safety is internal and doesn't need action from the shooter.

The entire issue of firearms is so polarizing as to be amazing to us. You don't have to write about firearms of course, but they are a way of life in the United States, so if you're going to include them, get it right. Many times we've heard statements like: "I hate guns", or "I don't like guns and don't want anything to do with them", from people who are otherwise open minded. Yet these exact same people believe knives, or arrows, or even swords are perfectly okay. The amazing fact is that edged weapons like knives, are used to kill more people every year than assault rifles, by a factor of five to one!

People (especially Europeans) don't understand (or don't want to understand) America's love of firearms. The truth is America would simply not exist without firearms. If colonial rebels had not had firearms for example, it's doubtful the British could have been defeated. Since the borders of European countries were firmly established prior to the era of firearms, those outside the U.S. do not have the ingrained affinity for them that Americans and newer countries have.

But this is not meant as a political statement, only a reality check.

Let's finish out this section with some firearm myths.

Can a .357 Magnum really penetrate an engine block? Absolutely.

So will a .44 Magnum and many rifles.

If ammunition is in a fire will it shoot off? Yes. But realize that the bullets will have little velocity and won't go far or have enough force to penetrate much of anything. A bullet's force depends on the tightly confined space of a gun barrel and the gas created by the gunpowder exploding, and all that is absent in a fire that simply cooks off the gunpowder.

Do silencers really silent? Silencers or suppressors only work to a limited degree and that is highly dependent on the type of firearms. Silencers do not work well on revolvers because of their open design. Silencers do not work on large caliber high velocity rounds because they just generate too much noise from the gunpowder explosion. The ideal weapons for silencers are semi-automatics in .22 or .380 caliber. The automatic pistol design contains most of the gas discharge and the smaller round mean less gunpowder to generate noise in the first place.

What is the effective range of certain firearms? In movies and films this is all over the map. Some will have you believe that a handgun is worthless over 20 feet. This is certainly not true. A typical 9 mm Glock can be very accurate out to a hundred feet or more in the right hands. And a rifle in .308 or 7.62 can be lethal out to a thousand yards or so in the hands of an experienced sniper. And there have been confirmed kills at over 2,000 yards with bigger caliber weapons. The trick is in the math: a bullet 'drops' or loses altitude over distance, so the shooter must calculate how much over the target (elevation) to aim in order to hit the target at long distances. Wind (and humidity and temperature) also play key roles. On a windy day the sniper must 'lead' the wind depending on its direction. That's why sniper must be not only patient but extremely intelligent.

One last point about firearm usage: a professional will never, ever, press their gun against another person's body! They will never press a gun to someone's head, or back, or chest. The reason for this is simple: the other person can usually react faster than the gun holder can pull the trigger. This has been proven time and again. And it's even more true if the gun wielder is a novice and their gun isn't cocked, since that requires even more time to fire the bullet.

Someone with a gun pressed to their back can easily spin and deflect the firearm with their elbow before the shooter can fire. At the worst they may endure a flesh wound, but the chances of being fatally shot are low.

A true professional will stand off between three and six feet while pointing a gun at someone. If you think about it this is very logical - for every inch of distance away, the shooter has more time to react and staying at about three feet eliminates the target's ability to knock or wrestle the weapon away.

And please... those scenes of victims cowering, digging their own graves, or kneeling at the gun holder's command so they can put a bullet in the back of their head, those just sicken us. First, if you know you're going to die why would you obey such commands? You're actually going to dig your own grave? Hell pick up the shovel and swing it - what have you got to lose? At least your killer will have to work and dig the grave! And if someone is pointing a gun at you would you really kneel down and turn your back? Fight! Fight with every last ounce of energy. It's called survival!

It's akin to those movies where a lone gunman holds 50 people hostage! People - that gun holds maybe 15 rounds at most, and if 50 people rush the gunman it's pretty darn likely he's going to get real nervous and won't be very accurate. Your chances are better than 50 to 1 to overcome him. Like we said: if you know you're going to die what have you got to lose?

Military

There's no easier way to make a lifelong enemy than by angering a veteran for getting some detail about the military wrong - and there are millions of us out here. So don't make a stupid mistake, do your research. Military rank is about the most critical detail.

First of all the Army and Air Force ranks are almost identical (because the Air Force was once part of the Army - circa WWII). The Navy and Marines (because the Marines are technically part of the Navy) use a slightly different rank structure.

Here are the correct ranks from lowest to highest - Enlisted to Officers: (Note the direction of chevron stripes are opposite in the two branches. Army chevron points up. Air Force chevron points down.)

A word about enlisted versus officers:

Enlisted join the service for a period of normally four years and are free to leave or re-enlist for 4 more years. They may stay in and retire with full benefits after 20 years. Enlisted Sergeants are often known as NCOs or Non-Commissioned Officers. Senior NCOs wield lots of power and are feared by lower ranking officers even though they technically outrank them. For example, a 2nd Lieutenant, fresh out of Officer Training School (OTS) is going to listen to a Master

Sergeant who is going to have vastly more experience.

Officers must be college graduates plus go to Officer Training School or a military academy (West Point or Air Force Academy). Officers generally serve two years and may leave almost any time after that. They may retire at 20 years or remain in the service if permitted.

To make matters more confusing both the Army and Marine have a unique rank structure called Warrant Officers. These ranks are in between Enlisted and Officers. These are mostly used for helicopter pilots and specialized skill sets.

The following pages detail the rank structure and insignia for each branch of the service. And by the way: in the military silver exceeds gold.

Army	Insignia

ENLISTED

Private Basic	No Stripe
Private	One Stripe
Private 1st Class	1 Stripe up / 1 down
Corporal	2 stripes
Sergeant	3 Stripes
Staff Sergeant	3 Stripes up / 1 down
Sergeant 1st Class	3 Stripes up / 2 down
Master Sergeant	3 Stripes up / 3 down
Sergeant Major	3 Stripes up / 3 down / with star

OFFICERS

2nd Lieutenant	1 Gold Bar
1st Lieutenant	1 Silver Bar
Captain	2 Silver Bars
Major	1 Gold Oak Leaf
Lieutenant Colonel	1 Silver Oak Leaf
Colonel	1 Silver Eagle
Brigadier General	1 Silver Star
Lieutenant General	2 Silver Stars
Major General	3 Silver Stars
General	4 Silver Stars

(There are 5 star generals but they command the entire branch of service or all branches in time of war.)

Air Force	Insignia
ENLISTED	
Airman Basic	No Stripe
Airman	One Stripe
Airman 1st Class	2 Stripes
Senior Airman	3 Stripes
Staff Sergeant	4 Stripes
Technical Sergeant	5 Stripes
Master Sergeant	5 down + 1 up
Senior Master Sgt	5 down + 2 up
Chief Master Sgt	5 down + 3 up

OFFICERS	
2nd Lieutenant	1 Gold Bar
1st Lieutenant	1 Silver Bar
Captain	2 Silver Bars
Major	1 Gold Oak Leaf
Lieutenant Colonel	1 Silver Oak Leaf
Colonel	1 Silver Eagle
Brigadier General	1 Silver Star
Lieutenant General	2 Silver Stars
Major General	3 Silver Stars
General	4 Silver Stars

Navy	Insignia

ENLISTED

Seaman Recruit	No Stripe
Seaman Apprentice	2 Slashes
Seaman	3 Slashes
Petty Officer 3rd Class	Eagle + 1 Red Stripe
Petty Officer 2nd Class	Eagle + 2 Red Stripes
Petty Officer 1st Class	Eagle + 3 Red Stripes
Chief Petty Officer	Eagle + 4 Yellow Stripes
Senior Chief Petty Officer	Eagle + 4 Yellow Stripes + Star
Master Chief Petty Officer	Eagle + 4 Yellow Stripes + 2 Stars

OFFICERS

Ensign	1 Gold Bar
Lieutenant Junior Grade	1 Silver Bar
Lieutenant	2 Silver Bars
Lieutenant Commander	1 Gold Oak Leaf
Commander	1 Silver Oak Leaf
Captain	1 Silver Eagle
Rear Admiral Lower	1 Silver Star
Rear Admiral Upper	2 Silver Stars
Vice Admiral	3 Silver Stars
Admiral	4 Silver Stars

Marines	Insignia
ENLISTED	
Private	No Stripe
Private 1st Class	1 Stripe
Lance Corporal	1 Stripe + Crossed Swords
Corporal	2 Stripes + Crossed Swords
Sergeant	3 Stripes + Crossed Swords
Staff Sergeant	3 Stripes up + 1 down
Gunnery Sergeant	3 Stripes up + 2 down
Master Sergeant	3 Stripes up + 3 down
Master Gunnery Sergeant	3 Stripes up + 4 down

OFFICERS	
2nd Lieutenant	1 Gold Bar
1st Lieutenant	1 Silver Bar
Captain	2 Silver Bars
Major	1 Gold Oak Leaf
Lt Colonel	1 Silver Oak Leaf
Colonel	1 Silver Eagle
Brigadier General	1 Silver Star
Lt General	2 Silver Stars
Major General	3 Silver Stars
General	4 Silver Stars

All of the above are basic insignia. There are different forms for ceremonial occasions and combat / camouflage uniforms.

Uniforms also cause confusion among civilians. All branches of the military have two basic uniform types: Dress and Fatigue.

Dress is equivalent to a civilian suit with a tie.

Fatigue is akin to civilian casual work clothes.

Some branches (namely the Navy and Marines) have a third, more extravagant uniform used for ceremonial occasions.

Dress uniforms are worn in office type environments. Fatigues are worn practically everywhere else. It's important to note that almost half of military personnel are not engaged in actual combat. There are clerks, mechanics, technicians, analysts, instructors, cooks, pilots, etc. Which uniform is worn in which situation is dictated by the commander. For instance, an air traffic control technician could wear fatigues or dress uniform depending on the local policy. However, you will never see a soldier standing guard in a dress uniform unless it's some ceremonial post, like say guarding the White House or something.

Fatigue uniforms can be a big source of confusion since there are seemingly endless varieties. The standard for all branches are the olive drab pants and jacket-like shirt. However this often changes depending on the global situation. During the Vietnam era fatigues were issued in green jungle camouflage. When Europe and the Cold War were hot, fatigues turned to mountain camouflage colors of gray and white. As the Middle East grabbed focus, fatigues turned to sand and beige camouflage. While plain olive drab is always permissible, military personnel are issued only limited sets of fatigues and if they happened to get camouflaged fatigues, that's what they wear, even if they're a state side clerk.

In all cases if the local commander permits fatigues that's what is worn. If they require dress uniforms for certain office type environments then dress uniform it is. But again, you will never see someone in a dress uniform repairing an aircraft or a truck.

Both dress uniforms and fatigues have their own sets of insignia as well. Green fatigues and dress uniforms often use the same insignias but camouflaged fatigues are always different - usually black to reduce visibility. Ceremonial uniforms are also different and use more elaborate insignia.

Oh, and those little ribbons? Ribbons can stand by themselves or represent actual medals, depending on the dress situation. (When you are awarded a medal, you also get a matching set of ribbons large and small). Ribbons and medals are only worn on dress and ceremonial uniforms. Ribbons also represent 'campaigns' - like a military presence in a country for some reason as humanitarian aid, battle, or operation. For example, anyone serving in Vietnam received a Vietnam campaign ribbon.

Rank promotions are based on Time in Service, Skill, Written Tests, Achievement, and sometimes decorations or exploits (Battles).

Time Line for Ranks

Private Basic	Airman Basic	Less than 1 year
Private	Airman	+ 1 year
Corporal	Airman First Class	+ 2 years
Sergeant	Senior Airman	+ 3 years
Staff Sergeant	Staff Sergeant	3 - 4 years
Technical Sergeant	Technical Sergeant	4 - 5 years
Master Sergeant	Master Sergeant	6 years & up
Senior Master Sgt	Senior Master Sgt	10 years & up
Chief Master Sgt	Chief Master Sgt	15 years & up

2nd Lieutenant	2nd Lieutenant	Less than 1 year
1st Lieutenant	1st Lieutenant	+ 1 year
Captain	Captain	+ 3 years plus
Major	Major	+ 10 years plus
Lt Colonel	Lt Colonel	+ 15 years plus
Colonel	Colonel	+ 20 years
Brigadier General	Brigadier General	Maybe never
Lt General	Lt General	Rare
Major General	Major General	Rarer
General	General	Extremely rare

While enlisted can move through the lower ranks smoothly, attaining the rank of Chief Master Sergeant may never happen and many will retire at that point.

Officers face greater challenges. In fact officers are often forced out if they do not attain certain ranks. And there are a limited number of officer slots as dictated by Congress, so many an officer retires as a Captain.

All bets are off in wartime however. Both enlisted and officers may be promoted on the battlefield due to attrition. And even in peacetime certain of the brightest and best individuals can jump in rank- for example a test pilot or someone with a special skill.

One important point: get the ages and ranks of your characters right! I have seen 40 year old men with one stripe and 20 somethings as Captains. Ain't gonna happen! If a person stays in the military through his or her forties they are going to be high ranking. And vice versa an officer is going to be in their thirties or forties before they get to Captain or above.

Another fact: enlisted personnel don't usually go around addressing each other with specific ranks. The person's actual ranks are only used in formal settings. Otherwise it's 'private', 'corporal', or 'sergeant' - period. 'Airman' or 'sergeant' in the Air Force. 'Chief' is often used in the Navy when addressing a Petty Officer. Just like they don't say : "Yes Staff Sergeant Smith!" They say "Yes Sarge."

Officers are called 'Sir' or 'Ma'am' by enlisted folks and usually no rank is mentioned. Airman and privates don't go around saying, "Yes Captain Smith." They just say "Yes sir!" Officers in a group will often address each other by rank however: a Colonel may address a superior as 'General'.

And, ranks do matter between branches of the service - a Captain in the Navy outranks a Lieutenant in the Air Force, just like they would in their own branches.

A side thought before we close out military - science fiction writers seem to have assumed and taken for granted that the Navy will rule space. Yes, we know they are called 'space ships', but how does anyone know that space won't be the province of the Air Force? After all, the Air Force puts up and controls satellites, not the Navy!

It seems just as likely and more reasonable and logical that the Air Fore would be the military branch to go into space - despite what the 'final frontier' would have you believe. So you might just want to break that movie and sci-fi tradition and have the Air Force lead the way!

Lastly, the military is a highly organized entity. It thrives on regulations. There are regulations and orders for virtually every conceivable circumstance. Nothing happens in the military without orders and regulations. If you fail to follow orders and regulations, you will be crushed like a bug.

That's not to say there isn't innovation and some limited free thinking, but ... only if such thinking is successful. If you buck regulations and succeed you will be a hero. If you fail you will probably be court martialed.

However, the military does prize ingenuity above all else!

Military Vehicles

Tanks, trucks, jeeps and other wheeled or tracked vehicles.

'Jeeps' were phased out after the Vietnam era and replaced by the Humvee. So don't use the term 'jeep' in any story set after 1985.

Almost all military vehicles use diesel engines, or in the case of the M-1 Abrahams tank - turbines. In any case these engines require oxygen to function. You can't use a tank or any normal military vehicle on the moon or Mars or anyplace without oxygen! If you're writing science fiction please just invent something. Only an electric powered vehicle will work on airless plants!

The military tends to go overboard on all its vehicles. When a new design is being sought for a troop transport or heaven forbid, a fighter, for example, they want everything and the kitchen sink thrown in. As a result American military vehicles tend to be overweight, inefficient, and have limited range. And even worse, because of the extremely long lead times, military vehicles are almost always built for the wrong type of war. This is why the Humvees were not the right vehicles for the war in Iraq - they had no armor and were useless in an urban guerilla warfare situation. Like much of the military inventory they were built for a war in Europe because planners can't seem to get WWII out of their heads. And all this is just as much the fault of defense contractors / manufacturers as the Pentagon.

Helicopters

These rotary wing aircraft are among the most interesting military craft but they do have limitations you must observe to be realistic.

The UH-1 Huey was used in Vietnam and later phased out in 1979 in favor of the UH-60 Black Hawk. They serve as troop carriers, medical evacuation, and gunships. 'UH' means Utility Helicopter.

The AH-1 Cobra was used in Vietnam and later phased out by the AH-64 Apache in 1976. The Cobra is still technically in service but is not used in combat. 'AH' means Attack Helicopter.

The Apache is about the most lethal weapon known on the battlefield with its M230 Chain Gun with 1,200 rounds and carrying up to sixteen AGM-114 Hellfire missiles. The chain gun (an electric driven multi-barrel cannon) alone can destroy most armored vehicles. But please note the ammo on these craft is not unlimited! You have 1200 rounds of 30 mm shells and 16 missiles - period. Once that's gone, it's gone and the chopper will have to return to base and rearm.

And then there is the range. Some writers seem to think these aircraft can fly anywhere. We just read a story where a helicopter flew at supersonic speed from California to Australia!

Not possible! The specs are:

Cobra - 315 mile combat range Top Speed 171 MPH

Apache - 300 mile combat range Top speed 182 MPH

These choppers can travel about 300 miles and then must be refueled. There's no way around that, they can't carry enough fuel to go further.

Any rotary wing craft cannot by its very definition exceed the sound barrier or even come close to it. Not only do the blades counteract air flow on half of every sweep, but most of the power is directed to vertical lift, not forward motion.

Fighters

The range limitation also applies to fighter jets:

The F-16 Fighting Falcon's combat radius is 550 km (340 mi) on a hi-lo-hi mission with six 450 kg (1,000 lb) bombs.

The F/A-18 Hornet has a combat radius of 537 km (330 mi) on a hi-lo-lo-hi mission.

The only difference here is that these planes can fly supersonic and can be refueled in the air. The American military has traditionally sacrificed range for every other capability, relying on air to air refueling to get by. But unless your character has a KC-10 flying tanker standing by overhead, your F-16 is going into the drink at about 330 miles.

On a side note: The A-10 attack aircraft is one of the deadliest tank killers ever produced but because it is older the brass in the Pentagon couldn't wait to phase it out. The problem was (as usual) they had nothing to replace it. Recently however, someone had a mind blowing flash of logic and decided instead of a new overweight fighter, they would bring back the A-10.

Even if you're writing some science fiction piece, range and other limitations are not going to change because of basic physics when it comes to aircraft. it would be better to invent something (not a rotary wing craft either) like a flying saucer that uses anti-gravity lift and cold fusion or something for power.

Don't let these limitations affect your story, use them as part of the plot. Don't be lazy and gloss over them. Use them to your advantage: Your intrepid hero lands every 300 miles or so and begs, borrows, or steals fuel, etc.

Spacecraft

While we're on the subject of science fiction we may as well address some other physics. Einstein's rule that the light barrier cannot be broken has been proved over and over. The problem is that the mass of the craft increases as it travels faster until 186,000 miles per second when it's infinite. Remember that famous formula $E=MC^2$? Energy equals Mass X Light squared.

In its most simplified terms it means no physical craft is going to exceed the speed of speed - ever. Many sci-fi writers get around this little problems with worm holes and space-time warps. Maybe,

maybe not. Frankly it doesn't look promising.

So what if faster than light travel is impossible? Doesn't that open up some interesting scenarios? It would take more than eleven years to travel to the nearest star that has a planetary system. That opens all kinds of story possibilities.

Or suppose it would take hundreds of years to travel to another star? Generations of people would live, bear children, and die aboard the craft! The journey would be epic. And once they got there they would be on their own for hundreds of more years.

Teleportation

A Star Trek staple. While there are some vague similarities that the common man could believe in, after all we can transmit sounds and images across great distances and reassemble them, this is a real pipe dream. Consider this: to 'teleport' a human that person's body would have to be broken down into seven billion billion billion atoms, transmitted by some as yet unknown means, and then reassembled on the other end. And what about that person's thoughts and memories? Would they arrive intact?

Such technology is not even on the most distant horizon. And even then, unlike Star Trek, it would seem to require some machine on each end - a transmitter and a receiver. And it would require computers more powerful than anything we could ever imagine to keep track of those trillions of atoms. Just not feasible.

Time Travel

Ah, the basis of so many interesting paradoxes that are extremely difficult to get right! How about a man traveling back in time to impregnate his own mother with himself?!!

And that is probably why there have only been a handful of time travel stories that were successful and stood out.

Most really good time travel stories focus on those paradoxes rather than the technology of how it was done. And we'd advise the same since the science is about as feasible as Teleportation.

But! There may just be an out for Faster than Light travel, Teleportation, and Time Travel! Read on...

Multiverse

The multiverse is the hypothetical set of infinite or finite possible universes (including the Universe we consistently experience) that together comprise everything that exists: the entirety of space, time, matter, and energy as well as the physical laws and constants that describe them. The various universes within the multiverse are sometimes called parallel universes.

The structure of the multiverse, the nature of each universe within it and the relationships among the various constituent universes, depend on the specific multiverse hypothesis considered. Multiple universes have been hypothesized in cosmology, physics, astronomy, religion, philosophy, transpersonal psychology, and fiction, particularly in science fiction and fantasy. In these contexts, parallel universes are also called 'alternate universes', 'quantum universes', "interpenetrating dimensions', 'parallel dimensions', 'parallel worlds', 'alternate realities', 'alternate timelines', and 'dimensional planes,' among others. The term 'multiverse' was coined in 1895 by the American philosopher and psychologist William James in a different context.

The multiverse hypothesis is a source of debate within the physics community. Physicists disagree about whether the multiverse exists, and whether the multiverse is a proper subject of scientific inquiry. Supporters of the multiverse hypotheses include Stephen Hawking.

So what does all that mean? Again in its most simplified form, the multiverse theory says that every instant of time from the beginning of the 'Big Bang' until the end when all matter burns out, exists side by side in parallel universes. The same goes for 'space' - all 'space' exists together in parallel universes. These are mind boggling concepts for sure, but multiverse is a treasure trove for writers!

If every instant of time, past and future, exists simultaneously, then the way we see it, it means under the right circumstances time travel would be possible. If it were possible to penetrate the barriers of parallel universes, then we would have access to every moment of time that ever passed or will pass! It would seem that an observer or possibly a traveler would be able to witness or visit any moment in time by viewing or traveling to any specific instant. The jury is still out on whether that person would be able to change time however. It has always been questionable whether the future could be changed (we and many others doubt it) and this theory would seem to prohibit that. In the multiverse one could observe time but never influence or change history.

If all time coexists in the multiverse, so does space. And if that is true, than suddenly forms of teleportation and long distance travel becomes possible in a roundabout way... Instead of conventional travel to another star system hundreds of light years distant, which would require many hundreds of years, the multiverse would enable a traveler to simply journey to the parallel universe containing that destination instantly.

And likewise this would make possible a form of teleportation! Instead of the impossible task of breaking up a human into billions of atoms and reassembling them, a person could 'teleport' themselves through alternate universes to their destination by bypassing 'space'.

These methods circumvent all the problems with Faster Than Light speeds and absurd 'Beam Me Up, Scotty' scenarios while actually having a basis in science. Just keep in mind that any such machine that would be capable of multiverse travel would likely require some sort of portal on each end. The pioneers may in fact have to make the physical journey so they could transport a 'portal' to some distant star system so that those that follow could travel there instantly.

Computers, Networks, and Hacking

Hacking is quite the popular subject these days as it is in the news everyday. The fact is that few people know what it means since the term 'hacking' has been completely butchered. As used in the media these days hacking more likely refers to someone guessing someone else's password so they can gain access to some celebrity's private nude photos!

Wikipedia defines Hacking as:

Computer hacking, including the following types of activity:

Hacker (programmer subculture), activity within the computer programmer subculture -or-

Hacker (computer security), to access computer networks, legally or otherwise - or-

Computer crime

At this point a basic understanding of the situation would be helpful.

Pre 1980's computers were mostly huge (usually IBM) mainframes in the basement of some university or government building. Users connected to them via hardwire with 'dumb terminals' (these were displays with no intelligence). Often these connections were over leased telephone lines if the terminals were remote, and later - modems. The Internet as we know it today did not exist. 'Hacking' was almost non-existent and no one was all that concerned with security. The worst that usually happened was some college students stealing valuable computer time. Still, it was becoming an issue - see the film 'Wargames'.

The next phase was client-server networks. In this configuration the mainframe became a server and the dumb terminal morphed into

PCs connected over Ethernet into a Local Area Network or LAN. LANs were interconnected over distances into Wide Area Networks (WAN) running over the same telephone lines with more sophisticated data structures. People paid more attention to security, but it was still not considered a major problem.

With the advent of the Internet and widespread public access to it, hacking came into it's own. The 'Internet' is merely a collection of WANs with an easily addressable means of connection known as DNS or Domain Name Servers. Prior to DNS a user had to know what specific server they wanted to connect with and its unique address. In the early years the Internet was limited to education, scientific and government users. When DNS was invented all remote servers suddenly became accessible (if the owner desired) - and this opened the door to hacking or illegal access.

Mainstream media would have you believe that hackers are capable of anything and we have read books and seen movies that depict impossible accomplishments.

To learn what is actually possible for hackers, you must understand one important point: there are networks that are not connected to the Internet and hacking into computers on these is virtually impossible - unless the hacker has physical access to the servers.

On the other hand, hacking into Internet connected computers (and any intelligent connected device) is possible. So could someone hack into your 'smart' TV? Yes absolutely - if it is connected to the Internet. The only protection against this unauthorized access is software. If the software has vulnerabilities a hacker can probably exploit them and gain access.

But hacking into non-Internet connected computers and networks requires the hacker be physically present inside the facility or network and be able to sit down in front of one and insert malicious computer code directly.

Some examples of such non-connected networks would be: hardened military LANs such as those controlling missile silos, battlefield networks, atomic power plants, government and private research facilities, and ATM banking networks.

Other LANs that are not Internet connected would be mobile, such as vehicles, ships, and aircraft when they are moving. To hack an airplane for instance, the hacker would have to be physically on the aircraft. The same goes for a nuclear facility. A recent case of this is easily researched: the Stuxnet Virus.

It is fairly well known that the country of Iran is attempting to construct an atom bomb. The USA and Israel would desperately like to prevent that, but rather than bombing the facilities which are believed to be located underground, they tried a different approach. A virus was written to attack the intelligent controllers that managed the centrifuges that refined uranium fuel. The idea was to have the controllers speed up and literally cause the centrifuges to tear themselves apart. The only problem was that these controllers are not connected to the Internet and the outside world. The only way to inject the Stuxnet virus was to have physical access to the internal LAN. It is believed that someone planted the virus on a thumb or flash drive and tricked one of the scientists working at the Iranian facility to take it inside. Once that person plugged in the thumb drive, the virus was unleashed.

If you can learn one thing from this story it's that if the CIA can't hack into closed networks, neither can any other hacker.

Connected to Internet = hackable

Non-connected = no way

Now that you understand the difference, lets go back to computers and systems that are Internet connected and hackable.

As so called smart devices (Internet connected) flood the market society becomes more vulnerable. Our homes contain not only personal computers but tablets, phones, printers, HVAC thermostats, alarms, electric meters, gas meters, wireless wi-fi, cameras, televisions, refrigerators, even light bulbs - the list goes on and on. If a device is connected, it can probably be hacked.

Humans always forgo security for convenience because we're basically lazy. And this is the primary way hackers gain access to supposedly secure password-protected systems. We tend to select passwords that are easy to remember - or write them down in some easily discovered place (like under the keyboard). And we tend to use the same password for everything.

The first thing a hacker will do is a brute force dictionary attack. Basically if your password is in the dictionary, there are programs that will try every word in the dictionary to discover it.

Hackers will attempt to guess your password from research. With Facebook so many of us have put personal details on line that it's often easy for a hacker to uncover passwords or 'secret questions' like the name of your pet, your mother's maiden name, your high school mascot, or the street you lived on when you were five.

You'd be surprised at how many systems still have the 'default' passwords from the factory still active. We recently investigated a utility where all the remote locations were using default accounts and passwords set up by the software manufacturer, like 'install and installer'. Using well known passwords we could remotely log into any of 20 locations!

Targeted emails are often used. "Click here to go to your bank and reset your suspended account." Guess what? The email wasn't from your bank, or credit card, or Fedex, or any legitimate business!

If the hacker is really serious and targeting a specific person or business, going through the trash is often helpful to look for clues or even passwords. There have been numerous instances where bold hackers simply walk through an office and search through cubicles for passwords to business systems. How many of you have post it notes with passwords stuck under your keyboard or even on the wall? TIP: prohibit this practice and SHRED everything!

Sometimes hackers will pose as city inspectors, like fire or building inspectors and unsuspecting (and naive) managers give them the run of the place. Tip: ESCORT ALL VISITORS and watch them every minute no matter how convincing they appear!

Okay, all the above is hardly 'hacking' as the term was originally defined. No, the above is all amateur hour and social engineering. Real hackers use sophisticated program code to get into a system. Things like SQL injection...

But it's not the intent of this guide to teach anyone how to hack, we are more interested in how to prevent it while informing authors how it is done in general terms.

Another area where employees can be of huge benefit is properly utilizing their eyes and ears; something that unfortunately is almost never done properly. By this we mean that employees must be trained to recognize suspicious activity on the company's property, challenge strangers and report incidents immediately. Employees will respond to such needs in varying degrees so each individual personality must be taken into consideration. However, often the training itself will be enough to instill confidence to act when needed.

Especially important is just being aware of what is going on around them and challenging strangers wandering around the premises. You may find this concept too simple to warrant further consideration but we have continually observed actual events where employees not only did not challenge strangers but actually assisted them unknowingly in stealing.

A company was experiencing thefts of laptop computers in a high rise office building in Westwood, California so cameras were installed throughout the floor. Within a week more laptops turned up missing. Upon reviewing the video recordings, we observed total strangers dressed in business attire simply walk through the tenant space until they observed an unattended laptop. They would them calmly pick it up and walk out the door. Not one single employee asked who the person was or what they were doing there.

In another case, a well dressed man in a business suit walked into a company and went into the unsecured computer room. He then proceeded to disconnect and remove the company's servers! After placing two large servers in a roll around luggage case, he simply walked out the door. The employees, in the meantime, were frantically wondering why their computers were down! This incident was also captured on video- and again no one challenged the man at all.

Professional criminals often take advantage of employee 'helpfulness' and respect for authority by posing as repairmen or inspectors and requesting entry into secure areas.

There are documented cases where thieves posing as fire inspectors flashed phony badges and demanded entry to secure locations. Employees failed to question them or verify their IDs. The thieves then disable key parts of the alarm system so they can return later after hours with tripping the alarm.

While employees should be helpful and courteous it is imperative that all visitors be thoroughly checked out before admitting them to any sensitive area. Further, strangers and visitors should never be left alone to wander unattended around company property no matter how harmless or important they appear.

Thieves & hackers regularly dive into Dumpsters. Even a Post-it note with a customer's name and phone number provides enough to begin a scam. Employee names, positions and work schedules are invaluable to con artists.

HIGH SECURITY FACILITIES ALWAYS ESCORT STRANGERS

They never let pairs split up, and never, ever leave them alone - no matter what the reason. Thieves have even stooped to faking illness, and then spending as long as it takes in a bathroom until the most vigilant escort gives up.

HIGH SECURITY FACILITIES ALWAYS VERIFY IDS

Most people do not take the time to ensure that a stranger is whom he claims to be, even at the risk of giving insult. They don't check the name on a badge against a driver's license, or call the purported employer to make sure the person is legit. This includes Fire Department personnel, Police, repairmen, pest control, fire extinguisher servicemen, Electric Company, Gas Company, and especially the telephone company.

Just because someone has a badge or a clip board or is in uniform doesn't mean the person that shows up is legit either. Thieves and con artists will often know service schedules or overhear requests for service and arrive <u>before</u> the *real* service person.

DOUBLE-CHECK E-MAIL REQUESTS

Thieves will set up a fake e-mail address and credit-union website, then send out e-mails claiming to be from the credit union's IT manager, asking employees to 'test' the new website by entering their own account and password information. They often give thieves all they need to obtain codes for the alarm system or even empty out bank accounts. This could be an interesting scheme in your story.

Bonus: Central Station Stories

Central Station: an alarm company monitoring facility

After a stint in the Air Force, the author got a job working as an alarm response agent in Cincinnati, Ohio. He worked there from 1973 to 1983. These are some of the true events of those years.

The very first time I walked into a central station I was both dazzled and bewildered by an immense array of buzzers, lights, meters, dials, and knobs. Phones were ringing non stop and two women were scurrying back and forth in constant motion, ministering to the flashing and buzzing like some electronic priestesses.

It was 1973, I had just been discharged from the Air Force and I was looking for a job. Over the next ten years I would get to know every one of those lights- and many of the customers behind them more intimately than my own family. By the end, I would also see those lights and buzzers disappear completely into newer technology.

In the 70's Cincinnati, Ohio was a beautiful city with a vibrant downtown where seemingly everyone congregated in Fountain Square for lunch and free concerts. Unfortunately, American Alarm Company was located further north in the "over the Rhine" area. It should have been called the "rind"- or the "behind".

Over the Rhine was truly the underbelly of Cincinnati. It spread from about 11th street north to the University of Cincinnati, which was in itself an area in transition. The neighborhood was run down and full of drunks, winos, and trash. Our little oasis was two buildings and a parking lot across the street from a bar and an auto parts store- the owners of which I would come to call friends.

I have often said Cincinnati was the greatest city in America – if only it was located somewhere else. The winters could be icy cold and brutal, and the summers so stifling air conditioning systems were brought to their knees trying to cope. Despite all that, I would come to love this place and American Alarm would provide the fondest memories of my life.

After having been in California for the past 3 years at Edwards AFB; Cincinnati was a bit of a change. I hadn't really wanted to move there but that's where I had grown up and where my family still lived. My mother insisted we move to join the rest of the family. I would have much preferred to stay in California and find a job where I thought there were many more opportunities.

So as it transpired, I arrived in Cincinnati in need of a job. My father was involved with a security guard company and offered me employment until I got settled. After all, what are fathers for? Like other young people, I had no clear idea what I wanted to do and like many others that temporary job turned into a permanent career.

In no time I was again wearing a uniform- only this time it was as a security guard. It just so happened that the guard company was owned by an alarm company- American Alarm. and my first assignment was to American Alarm working kind of a second shift. I was assigned there to respond to burglar alarms from 7pm to 3am.

Cincinnati in those days was a pretty tight city. The mayor and district attorney as well as most of the local government were Catholic. The president of American Alarm was also Catholic and knew the DA pretty well. American Alarm was in fact owned by one of the richest men in the state if not in the country. He owned a large bank, many shopping malls, and major league sports teams.

American Alarm as a result had a stellar reputation in the city and good relations with the police. They were the largest security company in the area by far and had well over 5000 alarm customers, which included some of the most important people and businesses in town. Although I never met the owner, we often benefited from his ownership with tickets to sporting events, concerts, and meeting famous people.

My First Night On the Job

After living within the highly structured community of the Air Force and benefiting from continuous, ongoing, and intense training it was quite a shock to be literally thrown into my new job.

In the Air Force I was an Aircraft Instrument Technician, which involved complex electronics and systems on widely varying aircraft. I had been assigned to the Tactical Air Command headquarters at Langley, Virginia; served a tour in Vietnam- (where I came under fire more than once); and then ended my enlistment at Edwards AFB in California. There I worked on some of the most advanced airplanes in existence- some of which I still don't feel comfortable writing about.

Edwards was the Air Force's primary test center and as such we not only had a wide array of aircraft but others that were highly modified for testing purposes. We had U-2s and SR-71 spy planes. There were even Russian and Chinese MIGs there – brought over from pilots who had defected.

Work at Edwards was challenging and stressful since there were so many things to learn and so many mistakes that could be made; mistakes that could cost a test to fail or even a loss of life. I was always intimately aware of my responsibility and tried to live up to it. I actually had re-enlisted once already and was planning on making the Air Force a career until I got orders to return to Vietnam again.

My first tour in Vietnam hadn't been too bad. I was sent to Taiwan on occasion from Vietnam as part of a team that ferried aircraft due for major maintenance. China Airlines had a contract with the Air Force to perform the maintenance at their large facilities in Taipei. It was always a fun trip.

This time when I received my orders back to Vietnam I was a bit older and more settled, but an even bigger problem was they wanted to send me back as a munitions specialist. I was in electronics- an instrument technician, and I really didn't feel like starting a new career field in munitions. Since my second enlistment was up in just 5 months I decided not to re-up and the Air Force was forced to rescind my orders. I served out the remaining months with a little sadness and left for good on January 6, 1973.

Despite all that, or perhaps because of it, I wasn't prepared for my first dispatch in the civilian world at my new job. It was a Sunday evening and the typical shift personnel at American Alarm was comprised of five people.

The shift supervisor, Geraldine, was a black woman with milk chocolate colored skin, about 30- 35 years old, with the biggest breasts I had ever seen. She had a great body to go along with that chest, she knew it, and she flaunted it at every opportunity. Since Geri worked nights she got away with wearing the briefest halter-tops that were legal. In fact I doubt they were legal. Her boobs filled those tops to capacity and spilled over the sides. Geri induced an instant hard on in every man that she came in contact with (at least the straight ones) and I must add myself to that list. Over the years many succumbed to that temptation – if she liked them.

The normal shifts at American Alarm were 8 am- 4 pm, 4 pm-12 am and 12 midnight to 8am. Since I was coming in at 7:00 pm, I would be splitting shifts. Besides myself there were usually four service technicians in cars and four operators in the Central Station on the second shift. When I arrived, all the servicemen were out working at customers so I had no one to ask questions or guide me except Geri.

That first night Geri was no nonsense and direct to the point of abruptness; somewhat a difficult thing for me to appreciate, considering her appearance. She handed me a small manila bag and an address and told me to go- right now!

With no idea about what I was doing, I ran down the stairs and got in the 1972 Chevy Nova that had been assigned to me for that night and took off towards the address- a jewelry store a few miles away downtown. I had barely got out of the parking lot when Geri came over the radio asking my location, "you only have 15 minutes to get there", she told me.

Jewelry stores are high-risk targets, and as such had high-grade alarm systems. UL (Underwriter's Laboratories) lists and approves alarm systems for insurance companies. In order to obtain insurance, it is required for high profile targets like jewelry stores, to install a UL Listed alarm system. The highest grade system is rated AA, and those types of alarms required a 15 minute response by police and an alarm company representative with keys.

Central Stations are tested and inspected once per year. A UL inspector will check each alarm record and the response time. Sometimes the inspectors would even cause an alarm with the help of a customer, and test the alarm company response. If the central station fell too far below averages, they risk losing their UL listing-, which means they would lose many, many customers. American Alarm was the premier UL listed alarm company in Cincinnati and a large part of their business was UL accounts.

My first run was successful and I easily made it to the location in less than ten minutes. As it was early evening on a Sunday, a police car was waiting for me. A little nervously, I unlocked the front door and the officers and I went in and checked the premises. Nothing was apparently wrong or out of place and it was chalked up to another false alarm.

Later I would learn a proximity detector on the safe generated the alarm. This was a device that could sense when someone just *touched* the safe. While effective when they worked, proximity or capacitance alarms were notorious for causing false alarms. As I gained experience, I learned to get all the information on the alarm and what tripped so I could be more prepared.

The next few hours passed uneventfully as I was dispatched to check on janitors who hadn't set alarms and guards who had failed to make their rounds. Around midnight the shift changed at American and a new group of people came on board. The graveyard shift ran very lean- only one or two servicemen and two operators. As it happened, a guy named Earl was one of the service techs and his wife Mary was an operator- and the supervisor.

Earl was one of those easy to like, down home, type of guys and we hit it off almost immediately. Tall, lanky, and in his mid forties, Earl was somewhat of a hot dog. He hated sitting around and craved action- either repairing alarms or catching burglars. If nothing were going on, he would cruise the streets endlessly, waiting for something to happen.

Acting as my mentor, telling me stories, filling me on personalities, and teaching me with such patience he would have made a fine schoolteacher, Earl was my rock those first few months. He also constantly talked about women and "getting some"- despite the fact his wife was a constant presence. This would eventually lead to some very funny events but we'll save that for later.

After a few nights of working with the various personalities, it was pretty obvious that there was friction between the service technicians and the central station operators concerning who was in charge. Although no one wanted to put it in writing, ostensibly the central station shift supervisor was over the service technicians. This apparently often led to fights and "disagreements" over what the field techs were to do. This all came to a head the following week.

Since I was new, I tread lightly and figured I was better off keeping on the good side of both departments. It was also easier for me since I was completely off the radar of the managers and powers that be, due to my work hours.

During the week I was introduced to a whole new set of people in both the central station and the service group. American Alarm apparently employed a lot of people who worked part time. The weekend shifts were mostly part time while the weekday employees were mostly full time.

Dean, Gina, Glen & Rick were in the central station while Rich, Tom,

Byron, and Steve worked service. They mostly had a halfway decent working relationship going although there were still some tense moments. I didn't quite know how to take the operators at first until I overheard some comments by the field techs. I came to find out the whole second shift in the Central Station was gay.

While the fact that all the operators were gay wasn't the big problem (although this was 1973), some of the field techs didn't feel they received the attention they deserved from the operators, and used the gay issue as an excuse to make trouble.

One of the rules was that the operators were supposed to check on the status of the field guys if they hadn't heard from them in a while. While I could certainly see the importance of that, it was difficult to remember to do some thing if nothing happened.

It all stemmed from an incident where a service tech had fallen down and couldn't get to a phone. Remember this was the age before cell phones! We didn't carry portable radios either – the only radios were in the vehicles. I admit this didn't hit home to me until much later when I would endure a similar fate.

So I walked into a situation where both sides were at odds with each other and it was getting worse. The field techs ignored the operators and they began to retaliate by writing up multiple service tickets on minor problems.

Alarm technology was very crude in the 1970's to say the least. Basically, a pair of wires –leased from the phone company- traveled from the Central Station directly to the customer. Electricity was sent over the wires through a meter at the alarm company to switches and tin foil at the customer. Yes, tin foil. Very thin, fragile foil was actually glued to the windows and was part of the circuit along with switches on the doors.

As long as the circuit was complete- the doors were closed and the windows intact, the electricity traveled back to the Central Station and the meter there read steady at 20 milliamps. If a door was opened (or broken down) or a window was broken, the circuit would be interrupted, the electricity would stop flowing, and the meter in the Central Station would drop to zero. This would cause a red light to come on and a buzzer to sound to alert the operators of an alarm.

In order to calibrate the alarm system, there was an adjustment at the customer end to set the meter precisely at 20 milliamps. It didn't really matter for all practical purposes if the meter was a little off one way or the other but UL did require that it be at 20 milliamps. When the field techs got on the wrong side of the operators, the first thing they would do is check all the meters (there was one for each direct wire customer, so there were over 1000) and write up service tickets if the reading varied by even one milliamp.

This little war resulted in hundreds of service tickets. To correct it the field tech would have to drive out to the customer and adjust the meter with a central station operator- who was constantly interrupted to answer other phone calls. They would make an adjustment, be placed on hold for minutes at a time and then have to make another adjustment.

This went on for about a week until the whole situation finally blew up.

Terry was the service manager at the time and although I had not yet met him, Earl had clued me in on his demeanor. Terry was known as a rebel and a hot head. When off duty he would ride his motorcycle (a Harley of course) and get drunk- usually along with one of the central station operators, I heard.

Evidently, these close personal relationships did not go a long way to alleviating the friction- or perhaps made it worse if Terry felt betrayed. That Friday night- the end of my first week of employment- the service tickets reached triple digits and one of the field techs on duty called Terry.

Shots Fired!

Terry roared into the parking lot on his Harley about 10pm. He was drunk, mean, and angry. I was downstairs preparing to start running some of the service tickets so I didn't see the actual event. But I heard it- one very loud bang from upstairs, where the Central Station was located. Having heard gunfire before in Vietnam, I recognized it immediately and my blood ran cold thinking Terry shot the shift supervisor Dolores.

It was a very narrow stairway leading up to the Central Station and I admit I hesitated, not wanting to face a possible killer coming down. Luckily for me, Terry appeared, got on his chopper and roared out almost before I knew what happened.

That galvanized me to action and I took the steps two at a time fearing what awaited me up there. There was a keypad on the door to the Central Station, you had to enter a code to unlock the door and at that moment it seemed like it took an eternity to get through it.

A flood of relief waved over me when I saw Dolores still standing. At about fifty-five, she was one of the oldest employees, and was not known for a sweet personality. Her face was both red from anger but also shock.

Looking around, I saw everyone else was still standing – but seemingly frozen in his or her tracks. Finally Dolores broke the tension by throwing down an account book and muttering "goddamn him, goddamn him". She finally saw me and pointed at one of the alarm panels, which was actually smoking! When I moved closer, I saw the meter was destroyed!

By that time a few of the other service techs arrived and everyone began shouting and screaming. Apparently Terry had walked in, looked at Dolores and asked about the excess service tickets. She had pointed at that particular alarm panel (called a drop) and told him it was reading 19 milliamps.

Terry then calmly pulled out his gun, took careful aim and said, "This is what I think about your fucking 19 milliamps", and fired a shot right through the meter! He then just turned around and left without another word.

The bullet did some major damage so a tech and myself had to replace several drops and some power supply components, which took a few hours. Dolores didn't bother to call the management but they heard about it anyway later the following Monday.

Terry was severely reprimanded but kept his job- experienced service technicians with management ability were damned hard to find. Imagine today, he would have been put in jail and the company sued for millions but back then in the 70's was a different time.

At least the event cooled the friction; the operators didn't wrote any more bogus service tickets for a while but tried to keep track of the service techs- while they in turn mostly listened to the operators.

Umm, Umm, Good

The next few months were fairly slow. Earl told me burglars don't like to come out when it's cold. So I concentrated on learning about alarms and how to fix them. Rick on the second shift and Earl on the third took me under their wings. Because I wanted to learn, they were more than willing to teach me.

Since I also was highly trained in electronics by the Air Force, it was very easy for me to pick up. Alarms were so crude compared to aircraft; I soon exceeded all the service techs in ability. Most of them didn't even know how to use a multi-meter (a device to test for voltage and resistance), and I had used one every day in the military.

In fact some of the guy's troubleshooting techniques were laughably crude. Earl for one had his own way of finding foil breaks. Foil required a lot of maintenance. Windows would expand and contract ever so slighting from the temperature or vibrate from traffic and cause the foil to break in hairline cracks, which were sometimes impossible to see.

Of course, you could easily use a meter to find the break but sometimes they would be so tiny they would actually make intermittent contact and be okay when you checked only to go open later when the temperature changed.

Earl had what he called his "cheater" cord. It was a regular appliance power cord you plugged into the wall. He would attach one end to the foil circuit and plug it into 120 volts with the lights off and watch the sparks fly where the break was! Tremendously dangerous but extremely effective!

We got a lot of calls for service at restaurants on the third shift because they usually closed late- 1 or 2 am. The staff would clean up and then try to set the alarm and couldn't so they would call. Everyone absolutely hated to go on restaurant service calls and I never understood why- until I went with Rick.

We always took two cars in case a UL alarm run came in so I could leave and handle it. So I met Rick at one of the swankiest eateries in Cincinnati, north of the university. The alarm control box and power supplies were in the kitchen area where the chef was waiting for us. Right away I began to feel a little queasy; the kitchen area was filthy, with food all over the floor.

We did some quick tests and Rick was sure the problem was in the power supply. He made me take off the cover. I thought he was just training me but I soon learned he just didn't want to do it himself. As I removed the last screw, roaches began pouring out in every direction. I'm not talking about one or two mind you, but literally dozens and dozens. Several ran across my hand and up my arm!

I recoiled in horror while the chef stood there like nothing was wrong, with no hint of embarrassment. We somehow managed to find a blown fuse, fixed the alarm and got the hell out of there- only to see rats scurrying away as we walked to our cars.

On the ride back I couldn't get over the roaches, I swear I could feel them crawling all over me and got it in my mind they must be in my uniform. When we got back to the office I took off all my clothes and checked everywhere but could see nothing. The rest of the night I was still freaking out and nearly went out of mind about the roaches.

When I got home at 3:30am, I insisted on washing my uniform. My mother couldn't understand why and she was already upset because she worked days and was not pleased at all the noise-, which also woke up my father.

I never felt comfortable in the uniform ever again and ended up burning it. After that I was damned careful when working on a restaurant alarm and didn't eat out for years afterwards.

Fire and Ice

While winters were slow for burglars and break ins; fire alarms came into their peak. You would think with cold weather, fires wouldn't be an issue but in fact the opposite was true. Not only were heaters in use during the winter, but also there were holiday decorations and people tended to stay inside more. Freezing temperatures also meant water took on a whole new dimension.

Fire sprinkler monitoring was a big business for American Alarm. Sprinkler systems are designed to put out a fire by dousing it with water. These systems are controlled at a central location on the property and alarms are transmitted to the central station, which in turn notifies the fire department.

While fire sprinkler systems are extremely effective at extinguishing fire, they also come with a huge set of problems. The biggest of which is the very water that extinguishes the fire! Often the water damage that ensues is more than the fire itself.

Normally fire sprinklers are static- the pipes are full of water but it doesn't move or flow. If a sprinkler head discharges, then water must begin to flow through the system; the water flow switch detects this and generates an alarm condition to the fire control panel. A water flow switch is a fire monitoring device designed to detect the flow of water through a fire sprinkler system.

The way a sprinkler system works is a sprinkler "head" has a glass vial with a special chemical sealed inside. This vial holds a valve closed or shut so no water is released. When a fire occurs in the vicinity of a sprinkler head, the heat build up causes the chemical in the vial to expand until the glass bursts. This releases the valve and consequently the water.

Once a sprinkler head begins discharging water there is nothing to stop it until the water is shut off at the riser. This is usually done by the fire department when they arrive at the scene. The fire department is in no hurry to do this; they are concerned with putting out the fire. As far as the fire department is concerned the more water that dumps on the fire, the better. Fire fighters generally won't turn off the water until they are absolutely certain the fire is extinguished.

Sprinkler systems in cold climates are further complicated when installed in unheated buildings like warehouses and some factories. Water can't be left in the pipes or it will freeze and burst the pipes. In areas like Cincinnati, sprinkler systems are "dry", they are filled with air which holds the water back below ground under pressure. If a sprinkler head goes, the air is released, this lets the water flow. An air compressor is required to maintain the pressure.

All these functions must be supervised and monitored. If the air pressure drops for any reason, the water would flow into the pipes and freeze during the winter months and that was an expensive catastrophe. Imagine trying to thaw out and drain hundreds of feet of pipe hanging from the ceiling!

So in the winter months, we had to be especially vigilant and response to fire alarm signals became high priority. We only dispatched the fire department on actual fire alarms; the service techs or myself handled all other signals.

Toward the middle of February it grew bitter cold as the temperature hovered below zero and remained there for weeks. It seemed like we were running fire alarms and supervisory signals every night- sometimes more.

About 1:00am in the morning we got a low air pressure signal from a warehouse on the north side of Cincinnati in a town called Blue Ash- a big industrial area. It was about 12 miles away so it took me some time to get there- especially with the roads icy.

That was my favorite part of winter in Cincinnati (I'm being sarcastic)- the ice. Ice storms were more common than snow. Snow I could handle but often it would rain then freeze leaving a solid sheet of ice on every surface- especially the streets. Between my girlfriend, and myself we would end up wrecking 4 cars and part of my house over the years.

Twenty-five minutes after being dispatched, I pulled into the parking lot of the warehouse-, which I thought was pretty darn good considering. Then I discovered our keys don't work. Dolores was on duty and began pounding me with advice- "Maybe the locks are frozen; are you putting the key in wrong; are you at the right door?"

The bottom line was, our keys didn't work so they had to call the customer- who as you can imagine was not pleased. So I'm stuck outside for over an hour and a half until he finally gets there. It has now been over two hours since we got the first signal.

The guy admitted he forgot to give us new keys after the lock was changed and then opened a side door leading into the warehouse and flips on the lights. We were greeted with one of the most magical sights I've ever seen. I wish we had digital cameras back then so I could have taken a picture; it would have been a classic.

Every surface – and I mean every surface- was covered with an inch thick coating of solid ice. Apparently the air compressor had been inadvertently turned off earlier, which caused the air to gradually leak down. As the air slowly leaked, water began to fill all the sprinkler pipes. As the temperature dropped lower the water then froze and burst every single pipe. This released more water from underground, which then sprayed throughout the building and then quickly froze.

The customer took it in for a few moments and then almost cried. The building was completely unusable and would be for weeks. It was so cold- and forecast to remain so for weeks. The ice needed to be thawed and then the pipes repaired and everything dried out. That wasn't going to happen anytime soon.

There wasn't much I could do so I turned off the water at the main valve so at least it wouldn't flow again and left the customer sobbing inside. I later learned that they finally brought in huge propane heaters after a few weeks and thawed out the building. What a mess!

The Smell of Smoke

Not long after that incident, I got dispatched to my first fire. It too was a warehouse but closer to downtown and 5 stories- two below ground and three above. The fire department had been dispatched quite a while before but now there were requesting someone from the alarm company to help them find some shutoff valves. We had a book on the locations of all equipment so I grabbed it and headed down there.

The term "smoke inhalation", is one I'm sure you've heard many times. I must admit I never thought much of it. In fact I often wondered how someone could be sent to the hospital or even die from smoke inhalation? That was until I arrived at that warehouse.

It was a paper warehouse and the fire department and sprinkler system had already put out the fire. It had started in the basement and got all the way to the second floor before they got it under control. When I arrived the firemen were just rolling up their hoses.

As I pulled in, a fireman told me to go downstairs and meet with the captain. It was bitter cold and already the water was freezing on the parking lot. When I entered the building, I saw it was starting to freeze in there too. Not ten feet into the warehouse, the smell of smoke hit me. Trying to ignore it I found the ice coated stairs and carefully started down.

By the time I got to the basement, the smoke smell was really starting to affect me. It was stifling and my lungs felt like there was a giant weight on my chest. As I walked across the floor towards where some firemen were gathered I felt lightheaded and suddenly started retching. One of the fire guys saw me and ran over, by that time I was doubled up with coughing and not able to breath at the same time.

"First fire huh?" He asked. "You'll get used to it in a minute. This isn't even bad, the fire is out!"

Eventually the retching passed but the smell was so strong it was like a solid wall. I managed to be coherent long enough to show them where the valve was and we got the water shut off. In the meantime the ice got worse and it was a treacherous climb indeed out to fresh air!

When I got back to the office I noticed in a mirror there was black soot around my nostrils and mouth. When I blew my nose, the handkerchief turned black. I kept blowing my nose until it was clear. My uniform smelled like smoke and I ended up having to get rid of that one too. After that I was a believer in how deadly smoke inhalation can be.

Years later when I was involved in designing systems, I would participate in a smoke test at a large mall, We had to install systems that would not only signal a fire, but also turn on and control fans and vents to evacuate the smoke.

To test the final system, we employed large smoke generators which would fill the mall with smoke and then the fire department would time how long it took to clear. The "smoke" was harmless – mostly carbon dioxide.

Despite having been in buildings with real fires, I still was not prepared. Once the smoke filled the mall, the sheer disorientation nearly instilled complete panic in all of us. You couldn't see your own feet let alone an exit. Once again, I was made a believer in the danger of smoke.

Burglars are Dumb

As we moved into April and the weather warmed, burglar alarms picked up. Often there was an easy way to tell if an alarm was false or "actual"- whether the alarm reset or not.

If the meter dropped once and then swung back to it's normal 20 reading, chances are it was a false alarm. It could have been a motion detector picking up a burglar but even then they usually tripped multiple times.

If the meter went to zero and stayed there, chances are it was an actual break in. The zero meant the circuit was open- either from a broken window or open door.

Not long after I arrived for duty on a Sunday, we got an alarm at a small warehouse located near downtown under the expressway. This one looked good since it didn't reset. Despite being the job for over two months, I had yet to run my first actual, so I was looking forward to this one.

The place was pretty hard to find since it was way off any main street and the area was pitch dark. After driving around and around for 15 minutes I finally found it- a long low building directly under the elevated highway. My usual habit was to drive around the building as much as possible before getting out and going inside, to look for broken windows or doors. Almost immediately I spotted a window that didn't look right.

Leaving the car running and the lights on in case the police showed up, I got out and made a closer inspection. Indeed the window was broken, and slightly open. Someone had broken it and reached inside to undo the latch. The windows were tilt up and I could see they were big enough to allow someone to crawl through.

Returning to my car, I called the Central Station and told them I probably had an actual and there was possibly someone still inside. A police car arrived within minutes- lights out, and silently glided to a stop next to my car. I told him I had keys and he said, "Let's go in!"

That surprised me a bit. All the other times, the police wanted backup and K-9. They never went in alone, even if I was there. This cop didn't seem hesitant at all. I unlocked the front door and he went first while I followed and searched for the light switch.

I barely had time to flip on the lights when we heard someone shouting, "I give up! I give up!" and a small framed, black guy walked into the light with his hands raised. The cop calmly handcuffed him while I looked around at the broken window to see if he had done anything else or had moved merchandise.

Part of the glass window was on the floor inside- held together by our alarm company decal. The burglar had broken out the very window with our alarm sticker on it warning American Alarm protected the building. Wow, I thought, our signs weren't much deterrent.

Outside the cop was putting the burglar in his patrol car so I went over. "Man, this guy broke into the window with our decal on it."

The cop looked at the guy, now seated in back of the squad car. "What, are you stupid or something? "

The kid looked up at us like he didn't understand.

"You broke the window with the alarm sticker on it, you moron." The cop told him.

"Heck, officer, I don't read too good. I didn't know what it meant." The kid replied.

That's when I found out burglars are stupid.

I also learned the police came in many different flavors- fearless and not so much. Most cops insisted on not taking any chances to the point of extremes. Sometimes I wondered how they managed to even drive to the scene.

Other cops didn't seem afraid of anything and took the most hazardous situations in stride. These guys I loved.

Marking Their Territory

The next few months I also learned a lot more about burglars. Not only are they stupid, but also they really do some weird, weird things. One time we got an alarm on a construction trailer near the University. Earl was dispatched but I went with him.

We often traveled together when there was nothing going on to back each other up. Some nights we were too busy and never saw each other at all but when we could, we always went together in two cars in case I had to peel off and go on another run.

This night was somewhat slow, so we roared north up Vine Street lights flashing. The city let us install flashing yellow lights in the rear windows of our cars in case we had to park somewhere with the cars sticking out. Earl quickly taught me to use them on alarm runs. Amazingly enough, other drivers seemed to get out of the way when the lights were on.

Earl's wife came on the radio and told us there were multiple alarms so we were pretty sure it was a good one. We pulled in the construction site with several police cars right behind us. Evidently Mary had told the police it was likely an actual alarm too.

The front door of the trailer was closed but the lock was broken. All the lights were on inside too. We all went in with guns drawn and were met with a horrific smell. Someone had broken in all right; they ransacked the place and then shit all over the desk- in huge steaming piles.

The police and Earl explained to me this was quite common. Burglars often left bodily fluids of all kinds (semen, urine, and even blood) as little gifts for their victims. We of course, left this particular mess for the construction people to clean up the following Monday. I'm sure it was pretty bad by the time they got back to work again.

There were other cases of "marking territory" but in completely different circumstances. The same gentleman that owned American

Alarm also controlled a large bank and the main branch was right downtown near Fountain Square. We had the alarm contract of course. One night we started getting multiple alarms on the main vault.

There were several police cars waiting outside when I arrived. The cops didn't think much of the alarm, figuring no one would conceivably break into a vault this size. But the police were concerned because the guard that was always on duty wouldn't answer the night bell- causing them to have to wait outside until I got there with the keys.

The vault was located on a mezzanine between the basement and main floor of the bank. There was a large circular hole in the main floor so you could look down and see the impressive vault, which extended from floor to ceiling. The shiny steel door was about 12 feet in diameter.

The police and I went in the main door and rushed over to the railing to look down. We immediately saw why the guard didn't answer the door- he was busy screwing one of the cleaning ladies.

She was facing the vault door with her hands spread and her skirt up while he pounded her from behind. Every time he thrust forward, the sensitive vibration detector in the vault tripped and sent an alarm! Another case of people not being too bright.

Shooting Ducks and Other Animals

All the night servicemen and myself carried guns while on duty. This was a constant source of discussion and concern to some of the service men and the company management. Every few months or so, a trial balloon would be floated by management about us not carrying guns. Every time we all agreed we would no longer respond to alarms, it was just too dangerous to go into some of these places unarmed.

Of course, we didn't have too much to back us up while management almost always had some incident where a gun was misused. The latest one involving Earl, unfortunately. Earl had been on an alarm run at a clothing store and as is so often the case, he couldn't find the light switches.

This was a constant problem. Many business owners would not only turn off the lights but turn off the circuit breakers as well. This made it very difficult for us to find them and turn the lights on so we usually resorted to flashlights only.

Flashlights were as critical a piece of our gear as our guns and tools. In fact, American Alarm used to give out flashlights to the police as a public relations ploy. Any cop could come over to the Central Station, take a quick tour, and get a fairly   high quality free flashlight. I used one of those free ones but other guys bought their own. I found out later why, but that's the next story.

So Earl was walking around this men's clothing store in the dark, with only a flashlight, at 2am, responding to a burglar alarm that had not reset. As he later told the story, he heard a noise in the back and went to investigate. Not finding anything in the storeroom he heard a noise again in the front of the store and assumed someone was moving around.

Running back to the front he swept his flashlight across the room and saw a man standing near the door. Earl said the hairs on his neck rose and he reacted a little too quickly, firing his gun almost before he realized it. Unfortunately for Earl, the "burglar" was a mannequin dressed in a $300 suit.

Earl was a good shot and the bullet put a neat hole in the lapel of the suit. Needless to say, the owner was not amused and Earl had to pay for the suit- a large sum in those days for someone probably making less than $10 an hour.

Everyone else thought this was great fun and endlessly kidded Earl about it, who got pissed every time he heard it. I took to keeping my gun in its holster after that, just to reduce the chances I would pull the same stupid boner.

Over the years there were countless incidents of things getting shot by one serviceman (or guard) or the other. In one case, one of our guys actually shot a duck. The customer kept the duck as a pet- and a watch "dog". Turns out ducks make quite a ruckus when disturbed and are often aggressive to the point of violence. Our esteemed service tech went in to check on an alarm and was confronted by the duck flying and flapping in his face. He promptly shot it- also accruing a charge of $100 to replace the owner's duck.

Certain parts of Cincinnati were rampant with rats. Often I would be behind a business in an alley and see hundreds scurrying around. Once I heard their bleeping and chirping so loud I though the city was being overrun. Turns out it was coming from a storm drain. I shined my flashlight down through the grate and observed a solid stream of thousands of rats marching toward some objective.

Rats, birds, and pets cause countless false alarms. Owners and customers hated hearing that we think rats are causing their false alarms. We had a guy named Smitty who often worked graves with Earl. Smitty was an older, overweight gentleman who hated searching buildings and consequently -rarely did. We could never rely on him to back either of us up or even be sure a building he checked was actually searched. That's why Earl and I hung around so much together.

Smitty was dispatched several times to a small manufacturer on the west side of town for alarms coming from motion detectors. Motion detectors are not exactly the most reliable devices anyway and back then they were really crude. State of the art in the 1970's was ultrasonic- sound waves transmitted and received back. If the sound waves didn't return in a precise time, the detector assumed there was intruder and tripped the alarm.

Ultrasonic was very susceptible to small animals like rats and birds and almost always that was the cause of the false alarms. Smitty reported on several occasions this customer had rats and they were causing the alarms. The owner swore there were no rats in his building so we were at an impasse.

This time Smitty decided to prove to the owner he had rats. He sat quietly in the plant until the rats came out and then shot one. When the owner came in the following morning it was hard for him to deny he had rats- since a dead one was neatly laid out on his desk.

Many of us in the field wished we could have been there to witness that. While our management took the high road and reprimanded Smitty over the incident- I got the distinct feeling of amusement when the event was discussed. It was legend for many, many years.

This cat and mouse game sometimes escalated to ridiculous proportions. We would tell a customer he had rats so they would go out and get a cat to chase the rats. The cat would then chase the errant birds that would get in during the day, so now we had all three types of animals causing false alarms!

K-9 Training

Although the Cincinnati PD had several K-9 units, we actually rarely saw one. The cops would always call a K-9 unit if we suspected we had a suspect inside but the wait time was almost always prohibitive. On several occasions, however I did have the "pleasure" of working with K-9 units, mostly with Earl.

When dogs were brought out and didn't find a burglar because they had already left or it was a false alarm, they became very depressed! The handlers told us the dogs get all excited and then let down when they didn't find anything

To keep the dogs sharp, the handlers liked to train them in real life situations so if they had time they would always ask someone to hide in the building and let the dog find them.

I had never been much of a dog person. We weren't allowed to have one as a kid and as I grew older I didn't much care. In Vietnam the dogs were trained to kill and I saw some pretty gruesome stuff there. Back in the U.S. a few of my friends had dogs and they always seemed to snap at me- probably knew I didn't much care for them.

So I knew dogs had a place in law enforcement, and I always liked seeing them show up on alarm runs but I wasn't about to hide and let one find me.

Earl, on the other hand, loved it. He was always up for a game of hide and seek, and went out of his way to make it really difficult for the dog to find him.

In every case I observed, the dog always won. No matter where or how well he hid, the dog would end up finding him. This was pretty amazing considering the K-9 officer didn't have any real scent to show the dog, evidently the dogs just tracked the scent of pure fear or adrenalin.

Earl did up getting nicked or lightly bit more than once. The problem was the cop would let the dog off his leash and if Earl was hiding in a way the dog could get to him, he was in some jeopardy until the handler caught up.

One occasion the police actually had to call the paramedics out Earl because the bite looked bad, but as it turned out, it looked worse than it was.

Why did he do it? Pure excitement, I told you Earl was a little crazy and to me this proved it more than anything else.

Around this period I began to notice reoccurring dreams. I'm sorry to report I have no good dreams, only bad ones. At least I never remember any pleasant dreams. But each bad dream is etched in my memory. Often when I woke, the dream was still so strong my mood was affected for hours or days.

I always dream in color but almost never is there any sound. Later in life I would have dreams involving animals and I often wondered if they were a result of these events with the K-9 dogs.

K-9 Justice

Although rare, I did get to see the K-9s in action quite a few times. I remember the first time was a furniture store a few blocks from the office. By the time I got there, the police had already called the K-9 because the first unit had found the front door smashed out.

When I pulled up the dog was ready to go in so I unlocked what remained of the door, swung it open and then stood aside to watch. As the dog was brought up to the door, he started barking and growling, excited to get some action.

The burglar heard that and started screaming, "I give up, I give up.'

The K-9 officer unleashed the dog anyway, which promptly bolted inside. We immediately heard screaming and growling and in a minute the German Sheppard was dragging a black guy out by his leg.

The cops stood around laughing until the guy was almost at the door, then the K-9 handler called off the dog that finally let go of the burglar's now bloody leg.

One of the cops must have noticed the look on my face.

"Just a little street justice man. That guy will be back on the street by tomorrow and probably breaking in somewhere else." He explained.

Not knowing exactly how to feel I nodded and kept my mouth shut. On one hand I was shocked and a little sickened. On the other I was glad the burglar got what he served. This pattern would repeat itself many times and gradually I came to accept it completely. It was them or me.

The incident that really changed my attitude more than any other came a few weeks after the furniture store. I was dispatched to a medical supply warehouse just out of downtown. The alarm had not reset but there were no police when I got there.

The area was really dark; it was way off the main street and had no lights in the parking lot. I drove around the building sweeping the rows of windows with my headlights and saw a broken window.

Like many times before, I got out and saw the window was unlocked so I knew there was a good chance someone was inside. Leaving the car there so the police would see it if they showed up, I unlocked the front door and went inside.

There were rows and rows of shelves as far as I could see-, which wasn't far with just my flashlight. There were light switches, which I finally found, but flipping them on did nothing, the place remained dark. This wasn't unusual; it seemed like every business owner felt obligated to turn off all his circuit breakers at the panel.

When I moved further into the warehouse looking for the electrical panel, I heard a distinct noise coming from somewhere within. It was definitely someone moving around.

Kind of stuck, I tried bluffing. I already had my gun out so I raised it high and cocked the hammer back, making it sound as menacing as I could. "I see you, come on out." I yelled.

All I got for my effort was more rustling noises. "I'm going to shoot!" I tried. No response.

Backing out, I went to the car and while keeping an eye on the building; I called the office and asked for backup. In less than a minute, two police cars rolled up and asked what I had. "There's a guy inside, I heard him. But I can't find the lights. You guys want to help me search?"

The two cops looked at each other. "Let's get a K-9 unit out here." One said. There was no way they were crazy enough to go into a dark building.

While we waited they wanted to know why I went in there. "You should have called us first." They warned me.

The K-9 unit arrived within 5 minutes. The dog was frantic as he could smell the burglar. The handler even had trouble controlling it. As they approached the front door, the dog was straining the leash and barking ferociously.

Once again, the burglar heard this and offered to give up. "I'm coming out officer, I'm coming out. Don't send the dog in. Please!"

The handler unsnapped the leash anyway, of course, and the dog shot into the darkness like a furry bullet. The commotion was tremendous. We could hear snarling and screaming and boxes falling and flying everywhere.

The cop got concerned for his dog so he went in with his flashlight and everyone else followed. By this time there were like six cops and myself concentrating light on the shelving.

A black guy was desperately trying to climb higher on one of the racks as the German Sheppard pulled boxes out from underneath him. It was actually quite an amusing sight.

The handler finally heeled his dog to give the guy a chance to come down. The burglar sheepishly looked around and climbed down. The dog snapped at him as he hit the ground and he made an almost fatal mistake and kicking back.

The K-9 handler promptly unleashed the dog again who sprung up and went for the guy's throat. The burglar fell to the ground crying and screaming as the dog grabbed his arm and dragged him out into the circle of cops.

As it turned out when the situation calmed down, the guy was armed and had a long and distinguished criminal record. A sergeant glanced at me and told me how lucky I was to be alive.

"Don't take chances like that again."

But the more action I encountered the more I craved it, just like Earl. Without even realizing it, I was falling under the spell.

K-9 Fear

Not long after that incident, I had occasion to experience something similar. It was a bright, early Sunday afternoon with plenty of light this time. I was dispatched to a trucking company warehouse where once again the alarm had not reset.

Being early, it was shift change for the police so I was on my own. After letting myself through the locked gate, I drove around the building and soon spotted an overhead door open.

The door was only open about 6 or 8 inches but it was obviously the cause of the alarm. Back then we didn't get individual alarm signals for each point of protection like you do now. Usually there was just one alarm for the entire premises and it was up to me to figure out what caused it.

After parking the car in front, I examined the door more closely. It didn't seem like anyone could have gained entry through such a small opening but it was possible a kid could get in there.

We had several break ins in the past where adults sent kids in first, through tiny openings and then had them open a door somewhere.

The other possibility was that the burglar closed the door after him and didn't get it shut all the way. Funny thing was, I couldn't see any sign of forced entry. The roll up door was just open.

I radioed in that I found a door open and was planning on going in but the office instructed me to wait for the police. They stated they were responding immediately.

In the meantime I climbed up on the loading dock and I was shining my flashlight inside to see if I could determine whether the inside latch was broken or forced somehow. The loading dock was about four feet off the ground and very narrow, about twelve inches deep. There wasn't much room to maneuver as long as the roll up was down.

Within minutes several police cars pulled in, including a K-9 unit. Before I had time to react, the K-9 handler was already out of his car with a leash in his hand. As he opened the rear door of his patrol car, he reached down to hook the leash on the dog's collar- and missed.

A snarling German Sheppard flew out of the car and straight across the parking lot toward me. As the cop was shouting to his dog, my brain started analyzing options. There was no place for me to go. I didn't have time to open the roll up door; and I wasn't about to jump down *towards* the dog.

My impulse was to pull my gun and shoot but I knew what a mess that was going to cause. K-9 trained dogs were not only valuable, but treated as members of the family by their handlers.

Of course, I didn't feel like getting bit either. My blood literally ran cold as the dog jumped towards me. I readied myself for some pain and decided to try to kick the dog off the ledge when he abruptly finally heeled at his handler's continuously shouted commands.

Lightheaded, and near fainting, I cautiously backed as far away as I could while the dog now meekly sat on the loading dock next to me. The cop came over and apologized as he hooked on the leash. "Sorry, she's still pretty new…"

We never did find anyone inside the building but I was even more damned careful in the future around the K-9s.

In the Dark

Not all the fear came from burglars or dogs. Searching these buildings in pitch darkness was always trying due to any number of circumstances.

One night I went to a factory. There probably wasn't much chance of a burglary in a place full of machinery, but I checked it out just the same.

Halfway through the building, my free American Alarm flashlight suddenly gave out. It was so dark; I couldn't see my own hand. Continuing slowly, a few steps at a time I swore, hit, and pounded on the flashlight but no matter what I did it wouldn't come back on.

Luckily, I smoked at the time and took out my trusty Zippo lighter engraved with the Air Force logo. Flicking it on I held it up trying to see my way across the floor.

Immediately, the flame went out. Thumbing it again, the Zippo fired up and this time I held it close to nurse the flame. A breeze doused the flame and startled me, causing me to drop the lighter. The weird thing was I didn't hear it drop for a very, very long time.

That scared the hell out of me. Feeling like a blind man, I was totally disoriented so I knelt down right where I was. Stuck without light and too frightened to move any further in the blackness, I carefully disassembled the flashlight and tried an old trick of reversing the batteries.

This time when I slid the switch the flashlight thankfully came on- revealing a black hole right in front of me. The floor was completely missing! There was just a large perfectly square hole cut into the floor with no guardrail or anything to keep someone from walking right into it.

I shined the light into the space and could see it went at least two stores down before I could see the floor. Evidently some piece of machinery was due to be installed there.

After regaining my composure, I was so angry at the complete lack of concern for anyone's safety I felt like burning the place down. First I had to get my lighter back though, which was now somewhere in the shaft two stories below.

It took me two hours to find it. I had to find how to get down through the basement and then search around through debris and rubble but I wasn't about to just leave it after bringing it all the way back from Vietnam.

After finally getting back to my car about an hour after that, I realized I had been in the building over three hours and no one checked up on me. All kinds of emotions flooded over me. I was pissed about the hole, I was pissed at the Central Station supervisor (Dolores) and I was pissed at the flashlight.

The next day I went out and purchased a $20 Maglite- the same a lot of the cops use, and from then on always carried extra batteries. Obviously no one was going to look out for me– except me.

For years afterwards, I couldn't help but think what would have happened had I taken another step and fell through that hole. Instead of having a cautionary effect however, it made me somehow feel more invincible.

Christmas Cheer

While Earl and I competed to see who could catch the most bad guys, normal routine continued. One incident, while it certainly wasn't dangerous, would embroil us in controversy for years to come.

Kentucky and Ohio are separated by just a few hundred feet of water near Cincinnati- the Ohio River. This narrow border became a gulf where liquor and cigarettes were concerned.

Taxes on liquor and cigarettes in Kentucky were half what they were in Ohio; consequently everyone traveled across the river to Covington or Newport Kentucky to buy such sin items.

During the Christmas season, that trickle became a flood. Businesses on the Cincinnati side would send trucks over to Kentucky to purchase liquor for Christmas presents. While authorities generally looked the other way, it couldn't be blatant either.

American Alarm seemed to have cornered the market on protecting scrap and junkyards. I swear every fifth alarm run seemed to be to such establishments, usually named such and such "metal" company.

We had occasion to respond to an alarm at such a place – on the Cincinnati side of the river- just a few weeks before Christmas. The police were waiting when I arrived. The alarm had reset so I didn't expect much.

After unlocking the door, several cops and I went inside and looked around. In a basement storeroom, we found cases upon cases of liquor stacked in a neat pile that filled the room floor to ceiling.

I was surprised the cops were so interested in this when we had burglars to find. But after talking softly among themselves, one pulled down a case and the others watched as he slit it open and pulled out a bottle of expensive scotch.

Oh no, I thought, these guys are going to steal liquor. Am I going to have to stop them?

As it turned out, they weren't going to steal it. One officer looked at me and explained there was no Ohio tax stamp on the bottle. That was a federal violation. The cops called the ATF (Bureau of Alcohol, Tobacco, and Firearms) and I had to wait for over an hour till several plainclothes agents showed up to assess the situation.

In the meantime, I had called the office, which then attempted to notify the owner. But they couldn't reach anyone. Earl came over to see what was happening and got there just in time to see several government vans arrive to cart off the liquor- it was all seized by the federal government!

The following Monday, the proverbial shit really hit the fan at American Alarm. I was "requested" to come down and meet with the president of American Alarm, the district attorney, American's attorney, and the ATF agent in charge.

The scrap yard owner had already been arrested that morning and his lawyer was threatening every type of legal action against American Alarm he could think of- especially unlawful search.

After having me relate exactly what happened, the consensus was we did nothing wrong. The owner had provided us keys to use in searching his business and that's what I did.

The case dragged on for several years. Every court upheld the search until it finally ended up at the Ohio Supreme court. I didn't have to testify but they upheld the search as well. As I recall the owner ended up pleading out to some lesser charge and never served any time but that started businesses thinking about whether they wanted to give out keys in the future.

A Year of Living Dangerously

That night seemed to trigger a long period of danger: accidents, misfortune, and weirdness. Not all the danger I faced was on the job. Often just leaving work at 3:30am in our neighborhood was enough to get you killed.

I can't even recount the times I would walk out the door and find people waiting to jump me. We were supposed to change out of uniform and stow our weapons before leaving the office but I soon decided that was foolhardy.

The first time it happened, I had changed and my gun was in my locker upstairs. No sooner had the door locked behind and I was headed towards my car when I heard voices, "Hey man, you got a dollar?"

Turning, I saw two black guys approaching quickly.

Ignoring them I continued towards my car but they persisted. "Hey man, we asked you nice. You got a dollar for us?"

I just kept walking but they sped up and were right behind me. They started to get nasty and I knew they weren't just going to settle for a dollar.

By this time I was at my car- a 1968 Dodge Charger I drove from California. I had my keys in my hand but knew I'd never make it inside the car so I slid the key into the trunk instead which I hoped wouldn't spook them.

As the trunk lid popped open, my backup weapon, a nickel plated Winchester 12 gauge pump shotgun swung into view and I smoothly grabbed it from the rack I had mounted there just a few days earlier.

The two guys backed off immediately, "Hey we didn't mean nothing!" and ran like hell.

Another night I was almost all the way home- this time in full uniform with my gun still in my side holster. We had managed to buy a house a few months prior with a VA loan. It was in Florence, Kentucky; a beautiful, up and coming rural area about 12 miles out of Cincinnati just off Interstate 75.

The roads were pretty deserted that time of night, especially in Florence, which was still pretty new. I was minding my own business when another car sped by me, then cut me off and pulled across the road, blocking my way completely.

This time I was pissed; not scared. Getting out of my car I saw three occupants in the other. When they saw the uniform and my rather large .357 Magnum, they burned rubber getting out of there. I often wondered what would have happened had I not been armed.

A few months later- two weeks before Christmas, I was driving my very first brand new car- a Toyota Celica, at Florence Mall. I had just bought the car three weeks before and was trying to get some Christmas shopping done.

Mall Drive bisected Florence Mall and as I was driving from one side of the mall to the other, a pickup truck broadsided me. It would later be estimated he was doing over 60 miles per hour- through a red light.

The impact sent me over a hundred feet down the road, flipped the car over at least twice and landed me on the opposite side of the median.

After blacking out, I came to with people all around the car. It took the police over an hour to figure out what happened. They thought they had two separate accidents and couldn't connect the two until an experienced traffic investigator arrived and matched the paint on my car with the pickup truck on the other side of the mall.

The cops hadn't believed me when I explained the truck had hit me. They all thought I should have been dead- or least seriously injured but I walked away without a scratch.

These incidents reinforced an attitude I formed in Vietnam: *"When it's your time, nothing can protect you; but until then nothing can hurt you."*

Although I was in the Air Force in Vietnam, it was still very stressful. Not only did we feel the pressure of keeping our aircraft flying in battlefield conditions but the Viet Cong regularly harassed us too.

Their favorite tactic was to fire unguided rockets into the base at all hours of the night. Some mama-sans would pace off distances during the day -when they cleaned our barracks. They would also help themselves to any alarm clocks left out.

The VC would then aim the rockets based on their calculations and use the alarm clocks to fire the rockets at later times. When we hunted them, they would be long gone. Luckily the VC were not very accurate. Everyone kept such a close watch on the mama-sans it was difficult for them to measure precise distances.

Regardless though, the rockets were a continuous nuisance. They were usually fired in salvos at intervals of up to an hour. Each time the first rocket was spotted, sirens would sound and we were supposed to run and hide in bunkers made of sandbags.

After about 20 nights of this, some subversives- like myself- began to question the point of this. Our card and chess games were repeatedly interrupted and our party time cut short.

Several of us began disseminating the theory that we could be killed anywhere, anytime so why bother to hide and quiver? When your time came- it came; if it wasn't your time, you were safe.

This philosophy was pretty well cemented one night when a rocket hit *at the entrance to a bunker-* while twelve guys were trying to get in. All were killed while running to take cover.

I began to apply this same thinking to my job in civilian life. After getting over my primal fear of the dark, I became fearless. The more that happened, the more I thought I was invincible.

This belief reached somewhat of a zenith a short time later.

July 4th

It was a beautiful, sunny, bright afternoon and I was cruising back to the office from an uneventful alarm run. Having started a little early that day to cover for someone, I was hoping for some action. It looked like it might be a slow evening though.

The street I was on was a main thoroughfare, four lanes wide and one way. Gliding steadily in the middle lane, I held the car at exactly 40 mph since all the lights were synched to that speed- and they were all green ahead.

Without any warning a car come from my right and broadsided me at a slight angle. The impact pushed my vehicle across two lanes and into a metal light pole ripping off most of the front of the car.

The two vehicles came to rest in a pile of such twisted metal they were almost indistinguishable from each other. Without thinking, I got out of my car and ran around to the other. There was a woman driving and a man in the passenger seat, both dazed and bleeding rather badly.

The woman looked up at me. "Officer, he wouldn't let us over."

That comment made no sense but I ignored it and replied that I wasn't a police office but I would call for help. Thankfully my radio was somehow still functional even though most of the dashboard was gone, and I was able to call the office for help.

After dropping the microphone on the seat, I stood up and it hit me. I was completely unhurt. Looking at the car, it didn't seem possible and I thought for sure, I must have cuts or internal injuries. I was afraid to look at myself and since no mirrors were still intact, that wasn't a problem.

Ambulances arrived shortly, along with several police cars. The paramedics thought I was a witness, not a participant. When the cops realized the other car was mine, they were stunned and speechless.

They finally insisted I go to the hospital where I was briefly checked over and after finding nothing wrong, released. John, the president of American Alarm, picked me up. He was very concerned, but not nearly as much as when we drove back to the scene and he saw the damage. Tow truck crews and the fire department were still working to untangle the mess of twisted metal.

The car was soon towed back to our parking lot for want of a better place. No one could believe I survived that, let alone without a scratch. I heard the other people had serious injuries and were hospitalized for almost a month.

People at work looked at me funny for many months and I knew that were whispering about me behind my back. I didn't care. I proved my belief that until your time comes, nothing can hurt you.

Exactly one day less than a year later, I was served with a legal suit asking for *five million dollars* in damages from that accident. The company was also sued for $5,000,000. My boss kept telling me not to worry but half the suit was against me personally how could I not?

For another year, I lived under that cloud until the case came to trial. The company had the same attorney representing both of us and the case was combined.

Our attorney didn't say much and I was worried. I was accused of cutting *them* off and running *them* off the road. They both came into the courtroom in wheelchairs for Christ's sakes! Everyone felt sorry for them because they were so badly injured; I, on the other hand, walked away so it must be my fault.

The trial lasted all of four days and we won after it was revealed the same couple had filed over 13 previous lawsuits for personal injuries- and were seen *bowling* the night before the trial while they were still supposedly injured and confined to wheelchairs!

The Wine Warehouse

Although by now I had personally apprehended over a dozen burglars (Earl was still ahead with 15 by the way...) I had never had to fire my gun. That would change this night.

Sharonville was another industrial area about twelve miles north of downtown. It was known for a huge General Electric factory where they made jet engines, and a large wine distributor.

This was my very first run there, in fact no one could remember there ever being an alarm there before- and this one was still on a break- it was not reset.

When I arrived there were four or five police cars from Cincinnati and Sharonville. After unlocking the door we all went in and searched the building, which was quite large and stocked from floor to ceiling with cases of wine.

After about twenty minutes of finding nothing amiss, the police left and chalked it up to a false alarm. I was about to leave too so I telephoned the office and told them I was packing it in. Dolores reminded me the alarm was still on a break.

That surprised me but I went out to the car and got my tools including a multi-meter and went back in to troubleshoot. The building had no windows, only doors and motion detectors. I started at the control panel and began following the circuit wires around the building, testing at several points. Everything checked fine.

Then I noticed the wires going through a wall! Huh? Why would alarm wires go through a wall? That should be outside. There was a small steel door about twenty feet away on the same wall so I went over and opened it thinking I would be outside in the parking lot.

Imagine my surprise when I discovered another whole warehouse! Slightly confused, I walked inside. There were lights on and the temperature was much cooler in here.

Hearing people talking and making noise, I assumed there were employees working. Either this was a different company, or the wine warehouse workers had forgot to turn the alarm off and were starting the third shift or something.

Since it was a Sunday night, many third shifts started at midnight. We often had a rash of false alarms at midnight on Sundays from workers arriving.

As I turned a corner, I could see a large group of men loading two trucks. Walking over casually, I was about to ask them for their alarm identification card when they saw me. From their reactions it suddenly hit me that these guys didn't work here!

One guy immediately pulled out a gun and pointed it at me. Quickly ducking behind a row of steel shelves, I heard a bullet whine right over me.

My .357 Magnum in hand, I returned fire and struck one of the trucks and ducked back. The burglars were scrambling to open an overhead door while the rest got into the trucks.

I fired several times and heard breaking glass but the same guy fired again. This time he hit a case of wine above my head and the contents started leaking down onto the floor right in front of me.

The trucks started up and went roaring and screeching out through the roll up door. I ran out firing to no avail. Outside, I got off one last shot at the back of the last truck and I'm sure I ruined at least a few of the stolen cases.

After calling the police back, we all felt pretty sheepish. The investigation lasted hours and they decided to write it up as if the police had been with me the whole time. That covered my ass too and as far as I know, no one ever questioned the report but I never heard any suspects were arrested either.

I once read somewhere that you can only dream what you have already experienced. That is, dreams are made up of events that happened to you but are jumbled up and rearranged.

One of my recurring dreams involves a concrete building that somehow has no walls. There are slabs of upright concrete and people moving among them. The people turn into animals when I approach. The dream always ends as one attacks me. Another case of events influencing my dreams?

The Ladies of the Night

Although Cincinnati was this great Catholic city, that didn't stop certain borderline professions- like the world's oldest one. Hookers were easily found any night near the corner of 12th & Vine.

As we almost always passed by that corner on the way back to the office, Earl & I were both pretty familiar with them. When we were stopped at the light, they would often come over to the window and ask for if we wanted a "date".

Almost all of them were black girls- and some were not too bad looking. That didn't bother me at all, having sampled chocolate love a few times in Virginia and California.

Earl didn't seem put off either. He continually talked about them- although I would have bet he never had a black chick. He was so funny though. When we were up in the Central Station and there was nothing to do, he would say, "I'm going to go get me one of those black hookers down on Vine Street." – To his wife!

"Okay, honey. What ever turns you on." She would always reply.

There was only so long I could let that go. One night it was particularly slow. Earl was back in the office getting coffee and I was headed back to meet him. When I stopped for the light, a tall black woman came over immediately.

"Hey sweetie. Want a taste?"

That was too good to pass up. I said no but I had a friend who always wanted to try a black girl. I told her I would give her $20 just to ride over to the next block and meet him. She was all for that! So she got in and I drove over and parked in our lot. After putting her in Earl's car, I radioed in and asked him to meet me downstairs right away.

I wanted until the door opened and then sped away. Earl ran over to his car and got in before he realized he had company. I circled the block and came back around to see what was happening. Earl was standing next to his car, begging her to get out. I guess he wasn't as brave when it came to love. He stopped commenting on black hookers after that.

Hole in the Window

The excitement continued the following week with a return trip to the site of my very first alarm run- the jewelry store in downtown Cincinnati. This time there was no alarm; we received a rather mysterious call from the PD stating they needed to contact the owner.

Geraldine had me respond first to see if anything was going on. When I turned the corner, I could already see numerous police cars and cops standing around in front of the store. As I pulled up I could see one cop had his arm up to his elbow through the window! He quickly extracted it when he noticed me- a fact that would later make me somewhat suspicious.

This jewelry store is on a main downtown street, almost directly across from a hotel. The front show windows are constructed of burglar resistant / bullet proof rated, *two inch* thick laminated glass- the same used in armored cars.

Someone had managed to pound a hand-sized hole in the storefront and I could see several items missing and the rest scattered around. This was pretty amazing since it probably took about at least 15 minutes with a sledgehammer!

As you can guess, the owner was not pleased. There was over $25,000 in jewelry missing. I often wondered if any of that went into some cop's pocket considering at least one of them had his hand in there. But, of course, there was no proof whatsoever.

Feeling I had to say something, I reported the incident to Ron and John, the management at American. They seemed to take it seriously but in reality I knew no one could do anything. For the first time I think I realized policemen aren't perfect. Naïve? Yes, but in those days I was still a believer in authority.

The Clothing store

The warm weather was back and so were the amount of alarms. On an early Sunday evening I was dispatched to a clothing store just off the main drag downtown. The alarm had reset so I was pretty casual in my approach.

Nothing seemed out of place as I walked through the main store. The rear was a pretty large warehouse- much bigger than I expected from the outside. It took quite a while to navigate around the racks and racks of clothes. Then while I was checking the doors all the way in the back of the warehouse, I heard a faint noise, coming from what sounded like the front.

Still keeping my gun in its holster, I headed back towards the front. My first thought was that perhaps the police had showed up and were knocking on the door. On the way I heard another noise, this time coming from my right where I hadn't searched yet.

In a quandary, I ran and checked the front door first. There was no one there so I doubled back into the warehouse again- this time with my gun out. With my pistol pointed in the air, I turned a corner and was confronted with several people standing there in the fading summer sunlight streaming through a row of side windows.

The hairs stood up on the back of my neck and a frigid chill ran right down my spine. There was a whole family- two adults and two kids- standing there holding hands!

My brain struggled to process this information and then I finally realized they were all mannequins. When I was able to breathe again, I knew how close I had come to shooting and quickly put my gun away.

I never laughed at Earl for shooting his mannequin again.

The Big Guy

Despite being at American Alarm for over a year, I was still meeting new people. It appeared people worked very sporadically and pretty much it seemed -whenever they wanted.

The Central Station manager was a gentleman from England, named Malcolm. He had been there over ten years I heard. He seemed to believe in getting as many people to work as possible. Nothing made sense since sometimes there were only two operators in the Central Station, while other times there were as many as six or seven.

One night there were six people on, including a very large black man named Tom I had only met once before. There was a small break room next to the Central Station where the employees could make coffee and I was partaking of some when I overheard Tom talking with another part timer.

He was recounting an unpleasant experience he had the night before when he went across the street to the 1131 Bar to get some dinner. A drunk who wanted money accosted him.

"Yeah, and the guy was big- as big as Morawski!"

Boy, I thought, that was like the kettle calling the pot black. Tom had to weigh at least 250 pounds. But it really bugged me. Going to the restroom, I examined myself in the mirror. It wasn't a pretty sight.

We had a scale in the office so I brought it into the restroom where no one would see me and got on. It registered 295 pounds! This from a guy who weighed 150 lbs. in Vietnam.

I went on a crash diet right then. No soft drinks, no hamburgers, no snacks, no butter. It took me a year but I managed to get down to 180 lbs. I continued to watch my weight very carefully for the rest of my life.

Terry & Linda

On another night I finally met another operator I had heard a lot about. Earl talked about Linda a few times, but it seemed she rarely worked or I had missed seeing her until now. She was worth the wait.

A petite, compact woman with a firm, lithe body and red hair; she was one of those women that just exuded sexuality. It was hard to believe she was married with two children

But what made her really special was her easy going manner and the flash of intelligence I immediately saw in her eyes. Linda and I would eventually come to have a strange and complex relationship, but that's for another time.

American Alarm was to be rocked by two deaths that year. Both would have a profound effect on my life, one slightly more than the other. At the times they happened, however, I would have no inkling of their importance.

Time was speeding by so quickly I barely comprehended it. In order to buy my first home, I was working all the hours I could. My day usually started at the guard company around 8 am where I would help hire new people and schedule up to 80 guards. Then I would go out into the field and do on site inspections and meet with customers.

In the evening I would work at the alarm company from 6pm to 2 or 3am and sometimes if we were busy I would just stay straight through to 8am. I also worked there every weekend from 6pm to 3am. Since I was rarely home or not working, I had no time for friends or family. The people at American Alarm took the place of my family.

One Saturday night I had just returned from several uneventful service calls and when I pulled into the parking lot, all the other service guys were milling around talking among themselves.

When I approached them, the mood was weird and depressing-unlike the usual jovial antics. A guy named Rick told me the news-Terry, the service manager, had been killed in a traffic accident while riding his bike. It had just happened a few hours before.

Frankly, that didn't affect me much. I hardly knew him, and besides everyone knew he was crazy. So I went upstairs and just as I was about to enter the code for the Central Station, the door opened and Linda came through.

Jokingly, and just to make conversation, I blurted out something like, "Hey, did you hear that idiot Terry finally got himself killed on his motorcycle?"

Dolores came through right after her and overheard what I said and shot me the look that could kill. The same instant Linda turned away with tears in her eyes and ran for the ladies' room. Dolores muttered something like "you moron!" and ran after her.

The whole Central Station was quiet, no one was speaking and the mood was too heavy for me. I figured Linda was just sensitive to someone's death so I went downstairs and lounged around in the parking lot.

Earl pulled in shortly thereafter and I told him what happened. Like me, he wasn't much concerned about Terry; but when I told him about Linda he looked at me like I was crazy.

"You said what? What's the matter with you? You know Linda and Terry were an item!"

That shocked me to the core. I replied I knew no such thing, so Earl explained they had been seeing each for most of the year and it was a very tumultuous relationship. In fact, the night Terry got drunk and shot out the alarm in the Central Station was because Linda and him had a fight. She wasn't about to spend all her time with him because she had a husband and two kids so he got angry and she threatened to break it off. Apparently they hadn't seen much of each other the last few months as a result.

There were lots of cliques among the Central Station staff. Dolores was like a mother to Linda and the two were very tight. Earl found out later that evening that Linda blamed herself for Terry's death.

Linda couldn't function so she went home and I volunteered to stay and cover her shift. She never knew that.

The Unrest

A good deal of the downtown area of Cincinnati was black-especially the area where we were located. Periodically every summer during the hottest nights, the surrounding population would go a little crazy. This particular summer we actually received intelligence from the police department that they expected trouble.

It didn't take long after a cop shot some black guy just a few blocks away. We planned on riding two to a car and I broke out my shotgun and brought it with us.

The TV news was full of incidents and we were expecting the worst. But like every storm, there's always a little humor. The customers were calling in and requesting we keep an extra special watch on their businesses. You have to understand that every business in the black neighborhoods seemed to be owned by Jews- white Jews of course.

Dean, one of the second shift supervisors, was a light skinned black girl. Her voice sounded nothing like a black person- especially on the phone. So the Jewish customers would call up and not realize they were speaking with an African American.

One was especially amusing. "Hey honey, keep a close eye on my store tonight. Those jig-a-boos are all over out here!"

Thankfully Dean was not easily offended and just told him she would. Today, that would probably have been grounds for a major civil rights lawsuit.

By Sunday night we hadn't really had any trouble but our service calls were backing up so we went back to driving individual cars.

Right after dark, I got an alarm run to a clothing store right in the middle of the worst neighborhood up by the University of Cincinnati hospital.

I wasn't afraid but I wasn't going to take too many chances either. The front of the store looked okay so I drove around back. The rear of the store was in an alley surrounded by tall buildings. Many building in Cincinnati, like much of the eastern United States, have retail on the first floor and apartments the rest of the way up.

It didn't occur to me at the moment I entered the alley how narrow and confined it was until I got to a dead end. I barely had room to open the car door but I got out and checked the rear doors, which were all secure.

An instant after I got back in my car something hit the roof. It startled me but didn't seem like anything to worry about. Then something hit the windshield- a brick. The glass cracked in a spider web pattern and while I watched that in stunned silence more items came pouring down.

Something really big hit the roof, and another brick shattered the rear window. Then a garbage can hit the hood. Bottles rained down and a few of them shattered the rest of my windshield spraying glass all over me.

At some point in all this I managed to put the key in the ignition, call for help on the radio and get the car started. As I attempted to back out down the alley, the tires were running over glass and I feared I would be trapped there.

Things were really getting grim as I burned rubber trying to back out but the rear tires were slipping on bottles and garbage. I finally made it clear just as a fleet of police cars arrived in a wave of blue lights.

Within minutes, the police were storming the surrounding buildings looking for the culprits. The whole neighborhood threatened to erupt in a riot while all the police pounded on doors and dragged out suspects. After an hour or so, Earl got there and that's when the cops finally found their men.

Imagine my chagrin when they brought the "suspects" over in handcuffs- two boys about seven or eight years old! I was so embarrassed I could have died but both the police and American Alarm treated it quite seriously. Our car had sustained over $3000 in damage and as one cop said,

"It doesn't matter if a brick is thrown by a kid- it could still kill you!"

River Downs

That summer was an extremely hot one in more than just the temperature. One of my more exciting alarms was to another of our famous scrap yards. This one was located on the river not too far past the local racetrack.

This night I got stuck driving the absolute worst vehicle we had- a 1976 Gremlin. Yeah, you read that right. At the time there was a company named American Motors, which would later be bought out by Chrysler, which actually made a car named the Gremlin. Talk about poor marketing! What were they thinking?

Since I came in later than the other service guys, they took all the good cars first. Usually this wasn't a problem because most of the time we had more cars than service techs, but during the summer months there were extra servicemen working.

The Gremlin was not only a horrible car, with no air conditioning but the radio barely worked either. Once you got about a mile away from the office it was worthless.

So I just made the best of it and left, even though I was pissed. I figured what the heck I'll just try to enjoy the ride and being out of the office for a few hours.

The trip took a good 30 minutes since I had to go on all surface streets and the traffic was fairly heavy. By the time I arrived, it was dark.

It was a typical scrap yard with a gate, which I had to unlock and drive through. The office was a fairly nice brick affair built on the side of the riverbank. The alarm had reset – or so I had been told when I left- but since I couldn't contact the office, I had no updated information.

In any case, after all the time that had passed since the initial alarm, I wasn't expecting anything when I unlocked the front door and went inside.

Walking through to the rear office, I still didn't see anything wrong until I flipped on the lights and found three guys- two white and one black- kneeling in front of the safe.

The light temporarily blinded them but they startled me as well. One of the white guys was first to react and jumped straight through the office window, breaking the glass.

The black guy went out right behind him while I grabbed the other white dude and wrestled him to the ground, figuring one suspect was enough- he would probably rat out the other two anyway.

My suspect was thin and scraggly, so it didn't take much to restrain him. After putting on the cuffs, I pulled him up and walked him outside. I immediately heard moaning and yelling around back so I pushed my guy in front of me and we walked around.

The first white guy- with a beard and long hair, was laying on the ground moaning, with what was likely a broken leg. Our brilliant criminals didn't realize the back of the office was about 16 feet off the ground because the land tapered down into the Ohio River.

The black guy was hanging by his fingers from the window ledge. After making the other two lay face down, I ordered the black guy to drop, which he did reluctantly, and made him lay face down as well.

At that point I was pretty proud of myself until I realized I was stuck. With only one pair of handcuffs, no phone, and no radio, I had no way of getting help with three suspects. The police had probably come and gone a long time ago. And, as I stood there contemplating my situation, I could feel mosquitoes biting me like crazy.

That's when the black guy starts in on me. "Hey man, you got to let me go. I was just trying to get some money to buy milk for my kids..." and on and on.

I told him to shut up and desperately tried to figure out a way to get them all back up to the office so I could use the telephone there. Not wanting to let any of them up for fear they would jump me, I was between a rock and a hard place.

The black dude must have realized my dilemma because he tried a new tack. "Just let me go man, and tell them you couldn't catch me." He tried.

"I might not be able to catch you, but this .357 Magnum will." I replied, as viciously as I could muster; while the bites all over my neck and face were really starting to get to me.

"I'm going to get up and run now..." The black dude was saying.

Fingering my Smith & Wesson Model 67, I was about to shoot him just to shut him up. My only thought was to leave the one with the broken leg lying there and try walking the other two back up to the office, but I knew the black one was going to be a problem.

As I was maneuvering around behind him, I heard a door slam and someone calling out. I yelled back, "Down here!" and was extremely relieved to see a cop walking down.

The cop quickly assessed the situation and after handcuffing the black suspect, called for an ambulance for the white one with the bad leg. Amazingly enough, no other backup showed up- either police or paramedics. Apparently everyone was busy somewhere else.

We ended up putting all three in the back of the single police car. The cop asked me to follow him to the station in case something went wrong.

The district police station was about five miles away but it seemed a lot farther as I struggled to keep up. The cop wasn't wasting any time getting there, as I'm sure he felt pretty exposed.

When we got everyone sorted out, the other cops and detectives at the station treated him as some kind of hero. What was I- spilt milk? I thought.

As it turned out the loudmouth black guy had no record but the white guy I nabbed last had been quite a busy boy. When the detective brought him up on the computer, there were three pages of arrests and charges- including burglary, rape, and numerous "assault with a deadly weapon" charges.

The cop that helped me out eventually explained what had happened and the detectives found a new sense of admiration for yours truly. One detective told me I was a very lucky guy I was still alive so I must have controlled the situation well. Little did he know.

This case would end up dragging on for many years. I often wondered why I was never called to testify but I figured they pleaded guilty or something.

Over two years later I got a call one evening from an assistant district attorney. He wanted to verify it was me and my current address. He told me then that the defendant's lawyer had informed the state I had moved out of town!

Another year and another call; this time they were verifying I was still alive! I replied yes, I was and then asked playfully if I had to fear for my life. The DA answered rather ominously, "I guess not."

Finally four years after the event, the case went to trial. Both of the white guys had gone to jail for other crimes and one had been murdered while there. The black guy was being tried. When he saw me, he decided to plead guilty and that was that.

Damned If You Do, Damned If You Don't

While I have up to now only written about events I actually witnessed or participated in, I'm going to break my rule for one story which I only have second hand knowledge about.

I have to add this story because it illustrates so well the pressure cooker environment of a Central Station, and the fact that it's very difficult sometimes for operators to make the right decision.

Ish was one of the day shift servicemen, in fact pretty much *the* day shift service. About the same age as Earl, Ish was very dapper and always neat. I never saw him mussed or dirty and never saw him with a tool in hand.

We often wondered if he actually had any tools. Earl had no doubts about this; he assumed Ish never did anything. I have to admit that judging by the number of open service tickets we had when we came in, Ish certainly didn't hold a record for closing out or repairing much.

The two biggest service items on days were fire alarm and holdup alarm tests. We were required by UL and national fire codes, to test fire alarms periodically. Ish would go around on a pre-assigned route and test these systems.

Also, since we had so many banks, the operators were required to call a percentage of customers every day to test their holdups. Often they wouldn't work or the client couldn't reset them so Ish was dispatched to correct the problem.

Now you might think this is a pretty easy job, and it was for the most part, but it did have its own set of pitfalls. The biggest one was that the Ish sometimes had the police or fire department show up at his location!

The two day shift operators- Shirley and Anne-Marie- had to keep track of Ish. They had to keep track of him so when he tested the alarm, they didn't accidentally send the police or fire department. Unfortunately, this happened all too regularly. Ish, and many of us,

(Ish especially) thought this was sometimes done on purpose.

More than once, while Ish was working on a holdup alarm the police would burst through the door and order him to the ground. Needless to say, Ish never, ever carried a gun- out of self-preservation.

The Central Station would always say Ish never called in and reported he had arrived; Ish would always say he most certainly did and they forgot to write it down. My money was on the latter.

After this occurred twice in one week, Ish was ready to kill someone and Ron B. the Vice-President, stepped in and demanded they not send the police when Ish was dispatched to a location whether he called in or not.

The following week, Ish was dispatched to a check-cashing place to reset a holdup alarm button. While he was working on it- two guys came in and held the place up!

Of course, Ish is frantically pressing the hold up button and the Central Station is ignoring it- per their instructions. Imagine trying to explain this to the customer –and the police.

Fear of Guns

My second summer was hot both temperature wise- and action wise. We were on the go every night and I was glad we had the usual extra summer staff.

One of the nice guys was Mark, a college student who worked at American Alarm during the summer to earn money for his tuition. Mark was bright, intelligent, and a great service tech. He was also meek and mild and one of his idiosyncrasies is that he refused to carry a gun.

Instead of making a big deal about this, Mark simply put the gun in the trunk of the car and left it there. Of course, we all knew this and endlessly kidded him about it. We kept telling him it was only a matter of time when he would wish he had one.

This was all in the midst of arguments from the management that we no longer carry weapons- and the fact that Mark didn't was proof we didn't need to either. So although everyone liked Mark, he was at odds with the rest of the crew and possibly making it worse for us.

Having been in the military I was no stranger to guns. Now you might ask: what did I know about guns since I was in the Air Force?

Well, most of what I knew was self-taught with the help of a few friends. We did get some minimal firearms instruction in basic training- with World War II vintage M-1 carbines. If I remember correctly, they gave us 60 rounds (bullets) and we had to get 40 of those- 66%- in a silhouette target from about 100 feet. A pretty easy task and I passed. That was the last time I handled a weapon until I arrived in Vietnam. So weapons to me were a necessary tool-just like a screwdriver or test meter.

As it turned out, Mark went the whole summer and never got an actual break inwhere he was alone. The police showed up on the only actual he had. Since it was his last weekend before returning to school, we all thought he deserved a going away present.

The Horror House

Dreams of buildings persisted, sometimes leaving me wet with sweat when I awoke. For some reason I never connected these dreams with my job. The dreams were so different from reality. Another dream takes place at a large house. I either own it or live there, I don't know which.

The house is very old and has many rooms. There are so many rooms, I have never visited them all. The rooms are filled with objects and antiques- and some people. People I don't know, and that frighten me.

Some of the rooms can only be reached by going all the way to the basement and then up other stairs and narrow passageways. The house has many stairs and halls, some are very tiny; all are filled with debris and crumbling stone.

The entire dream consists of me trying to find my way through to different rooms but there is such a dread and foreboding about what I will find I don't want to make the journey.

Back in the real world, there was one account where no one wanted to go. Even Earl and I dreaded the place and hated even going together, it was so bad.

The "furniture warehouse" was a huge wood building next to the railroad tracks. It was built on the side of a hill and stretched from the loading dock, right on the tracks, to five stories high. The structure resembled a pyramid, sort of, with the bottom floors extending a hundred feet in length but as it got higher the floors were shorter. On the upper floor there was another entrance off the main road where most people entered for business.

Once inside the place was a maze. Every possible inch was stuffed with furniture, floor to ceiling. Each section was separated by huge sliding fire doors that reminded me of entrances to dungeons or something.

The illusion of a dungeon was enhanced by the wood beam

construction and limited lighting. Light switches were mostly impossible to find but even when you got lucky, the only light would be a bare bulb every 50 feet or so.

The alarm consisted of contact switches on each sliding door and motion detectors at the end of each floor. Birds lived in this vast structure (and probably quite a few other creatures) so the motion detectors went off pretty frequently. We petitioned the management more than once to drop this customer but they never believed us about how bad it was.

There had been numerous break ins there but searching the building was nearly impossible without several K-9 units. We could have had a National Guard company and wouldn't have been able to search everywhere. In fact, there could have been a Russian Army company in there and National Guard companies looking for them and the two still have not seen each other.

So of course we decided this was the perfect place to scare Mark into carrying a gun. He had not had the fortune of ever going there before so I volunteered to spring the trap.

The plan was to have the Central Station dispatch us on a non-existent alarm. I would agree to go with Mark while the other guys would come in after us and hide. At the right moment I would "get separated" from Mark and the guys would start making noises like burglars.

We waited till just after 11pm when Mark had an hour left on his shift. Like clockwork he got the call to check on an alarm at the furniture warehouse. Waiting outside in the parking lot, I kindly asked him if he wanted me to go along. Mark had heard the stories so he quickly agreed.

With Mark following in his car, I led us down to the bottom entrance by the train tracks so he could get the full impact of what we were facing. I could see the hesitation in his face but he gulped it down and we went inside.

With only flashlights (I told him I didn't know where the lights were), we walked the length of the first floor as I showed him the motion detectors and then went through the first sliding door.

The doors had huge weights on a rope so they closed with a slam behind us -with a cringe inducing finality. On all the previous break ins the alarm had reset because those doors always closed.

For close to thirty minutes we worked our way upward; down the narrow pathways between furniture boxes, through the massive doors and up rickety wooden stairs. Of course there were all kinds of noises- creaks and groans of the building settling, trains passing, and occasionally birds flying around.

Mark pointed out one of them with a flashlight and he's the one who discovered something pretty horrible- they weren't birds but bats! So by the time we got to the top floor even I was totally creeped out.

I began to wonder when the boys would show themselves but I figured they'd hit us on the way out. I had Mark search the rest of the top floor when I heard some noises and started grinning to myself- let the fun begin!

Instead of retracing our steps we took the stairs on the opposite end of the building. When we reached the next floor down I shined my flashlight up on a beam to show Mark where the motion detector was located.

Only trouble was- the motion detector was gone, there were only cut wires in its place! Mark looked at me in the near total darkness, "Are you sure that's where it was?"

Shining my light at the empty spot again, I replied. "Yeah, I'm sure." But I actually thought those idiots had purposely removed it. This was going a little too far I thought.

Mark was really on edge by now. I was calm and he thought I was some macho hero. "Man, I can't believe this. Don't you think we need to get out of here?" He asked.

"Well, we at least need to fix it. That's for sure."

"I can't believe you're so calm. The burglars could still be in here."

That's when we heard more noises below us. I figured the boys were really putting on a show. Mark and I started down, he was going much more quickly than I wanted but I couldn't get him to slow down. I was afraid the guys wouldn't have a chance to make more fun.

Within ten minutes we were back outside. Expecting to see my fellow merry makers, I was surprised to be faced with an empty parking lot. Mark was visibly shaking so I let him calm down a little while I got on the radio. Geraldine apologized, she said they got busy and the guys couldn't come and we'd have to wait for next year!

Not sure if she was pulling my leg, I suspected I was being set up too. I figured the guys were parked up top and continuing on with the joke -except including me in it.

To test the waters, I asked for police backup, telling them we had a potential burglar still inside. Geraldine confirmed she would call them.

Five minutes later the police showed up. So it wasn't a joke! There had been burglars inside with us the whole time! The cops brought a K-9 unit and they searched for over an hour but found nothing except some multiple scents. I had to drive back to the office to pick up the part and spent several hours changing it- by myself- in the dark.

Mysteriously enough, Mark did not return the following summer.

Dayton or Die

Perhaps that's a wee bit dramatic but a trip to Dayton did cap off the summer. Speeding was a way of life for us- especially Earl and I. Our cars had the yellow flashing lights in the rear window which didn't entitle us to anything. We were supposed to observe all the rules of the road.

Exactly how much we got away with strictly depended on the individual cop. The police in the early evenings were not to be messed with; but as the night grew into morning we were able to get away with almost anything.

Sometimes when I was on my way to an alarm and going a little faster than I should have, a cop would pull up along side and tell me to slow down. Other cops would pull up along side and tell me to speed it up!

Once Earl and I were traveling at a pretty good clip straight up Vine Street, with the yellow lights flashing; when a police car sped up from behind with blue lights and siren.

I thought, oh man we're going to get nailed with a ticket this time for sure. Earl didn't let up so I didn't either. The squad car pulled next to us and yelled, "You going to that alarm?"

I nodded meekly and he waved us on, "Well come on then!"

We immediately went from about 50 mph to over 80 mph and got there in time to see people carrying televisions out of the store. All hell broke loose and the three of us split up to chase down the burglars.

Earl seemed to know every cop in Cincinnati but when we got out of the city, he was on less sure ground. That didn't slow him down much though.

One night we were heading up Interstate 71 to a distant location. I-71 was pretty new back then and lightly traveled. We were doing about 80 or 85 mph when a county sheriff came up behind us with lights flashing.

The cop pulled around me and got right on Earl's tail. Earl then pulls over in the middle of the Interstate, gets out of the car and puts his hands up.

I'm thinking, "Oh shit! We're going to be thrown in jail."

The cop jumps out of his police car laughing so hard he started to cry. Turns out Earl knew him too.

But I eventually got the better of Earl and held the all time speed record for quite a while.

American Alarm had its main office in Cincinnati and a branch office in Indianapolis. We had lots of business but never seemed able to penetrate the Dayton, Ohio market- 50 miles away.

American Alarm had a salesman named Rick who was pretty well liked and a little crazy. He sometimes came in at night to go on alarm runs to see what happened. He claimed it made him understand the business better.

Rick got to be pretty successful and signed up a major furrier in Cincinnati. Furs were high value, of course, so they required a UL alarm. The client ended up liking us a lot and asked Rick to put a system in his new store in Dayton. Trouble was, we didn't have any UL accounts in Dayton because it was considered too far away.

UL breaks their alarm listings into three categories: A, B & C. Grade A required a 15 minute response, Grade B – 20, and Grade C was 30 minutes. So Rick came in one night and asked what we could do about this. I should say he *challenged* us to do something about this.

Obviously, Grade A or B was out of the question; but Grade C in 30 minutes? At 100 mph, we could conceivably make the 50 miles in 30 minutes- but that would require an *average* of 100 miles per hour!

Rick was offering $100 to whoever could make the run. It was either Earl or me; we were the only ones crazy enough to attempt it. Earl wanted to go so bad but his wife found out and nixed that idea, so it came down to me.

I must post a disclaimer- the management of American Alarm did not sanction this attempt. In fact they knew nothing about it. Rick figured we'd tell them if we were successful.

We planned it for the following Sunday evening. Rick would ride shotgun- which I welcomed. I consulted maps and figured the I-71 to I-275 would be a tiny bit further but much faster since there was no traffic on those roads- especially on Sunday night. I would then have to cut over to I-75 and that might be our downfall.

The unwritten rule for UL response time was that you could take a running start and then call in your arrival when the account was in sight. In other words we would be in the car, in front of our building with the engine running; and when we could see the store we would count that as arriving.

All the service techs and operators gathered outside to see us off, except for Earl's wife, who would time stamp an alarm ticket. She seemed all right with it now that her husband wasn't risking *his* neck!

I thumbed the radio mic and accelerated away, down Race Street, around the corner and onto the expressway. It was a smooth ride once we got onto Interstate 71 as I sped up to the car's maximum speed- about 125 mph. We had Chevy Novas at the time- with 350 cubic inch V-8s in them. We were in Unit #4- the newest and best of the fleet.

We made the circle over I-275 without problems and then onto the well traveled Interstate 75. This night it was filled with trucks but very few cars. Luckily the trucks stayed to the right. Rick brought his CB radio (really big at the time- remember the song "Convoy") so he could monitor the trucker's comments. We were afraid one of them would call the State Police.

It was a wild ride. Occasionally I swerved in and out around slower vehicles, but I kept my foot to the floor trying to maintain that 100 mph average.

We heard plenty of chatter over the CB. Truckers would be yelling, "Did you see that!" and

"Watch out, here comes a fast mover!"

Once or twice a trucker would talk about notifying the cops but Rick would get on the CB and talk them out of it. The whole entire fifty miles, we didn't see a single police car.

Rick knew exactly where the fur store was located so he described the best route. When we took the exit ramp the clock had run up to 25 minutes!

Two corners at high speed and we were on the street where the store was located. The instant Rick made out the customer's sign we called it in: 10-97 – arrival on location.

We made it in exactly 28 minutes- 2 minutes to spare! I pocketed a very sweet $100 and bragging rights to the fastest alarm response at American Alarm.

The Psychological Stress Evaluator

While I had so much fun at American Alarm, I was also working a full time job at the guard company. This got very interesting with various clients such as Proctor and Gamble and Kenner Toys.

The guard division was often asked to do investigations but only my father had any experience and he was busy just trying to hire guards and fill positions.

Somehow he heard about a company named Dektor, who had invented a new kind of lie detector called the PSE or Psychological Stress Evaluator. It was pretty expensive- something in the neighborhood of $10,000, but John the president of American Alarm, thought it would be a great tool to get us in the investigation business.

The PSE required specialized training so I was sent to Fairfax, Virginia for a week. I swear the whole company was run by spooks. The trainer was a psychologist and a master in getting into your head. Some of the other people in class wouldn't even tell me where they worked.

The training was one of the most fascinating trips into the human psyche I ever got the opportunity to take. The lessons I learned, I continue to utilize to this day and I came back a true believer in the PSE. In fact, the PSE would prove to be so accurate it was depressing.

The machine consisted of a very elaborate tape recorder built into a black box with the PSE circuitry and a paper tape graph. The PSE was designed to detect micro-stress in the vocal cords of a person who was lying. You would record the person answering questions and then play back the audio through the machine. The PSE would then display the results on the paper graph which looked very much like the traditional lie detector.

If a person was truthful, the theory was that the recorded audio of their voice would be relaxed- like a gentle wave pattern. If the person was lying, the vocal pattern would be dense and bunched up.

The biggest advantage of the PSE was that it only required a voice recording- no wires needed to be connected to the suspect. That meant the machine could be used *over the phone*- a fact continually pointed out by the instructors.

The technique we were taught was simple. Ask a series of baseline non-pertinent yes or no questions, like "Is your hair black?" "Is your mother's name Ann?" These would establish a person's normal level and baseline pattern.

Then you would ask the real questions and compare those results with the baseline. In most of my experiences with the machine, it was ridiculously easy to tell lies from truth.

The instructor carried the whole process a bit farther for "advanced" users. He combined his psychological training with the supposedly non- pertinent questions to develop even more information about the suspect's personality.

One of his favorite tricks was to use questions about colors. He would ask, "What is your favorite color?"

If the person replied "Black", that was supposed to be a death wish. "Green" (being the color of money) would indicate a strong preference for riches and would indicate that person might be a strong suspect if the investigation concerned money.

"Blue" is relaxing, "Red" is exciting, "Yellow" is bright but neutral and yielding- all keys to the person's personality if used correctly. Although I was only exposed to this for a week, I continued to study this for many years and found it to be a very viable avenue to understanding people in all circumstances.

My first case with the PSE involved a client of the guard company- a large toy manufacturer. The company had a highly sought after series of action figures that had not yet been released; but they were turning up in flea markets around Cincinnati.

Our company had 18 guards assigned there on various shifts so the company wanted them cleared first. As far as we knew, none were suspected. We thought they were all good guys, especially the field supervisor, who was one of our very best guards.

The scenario we planned to use was to interview each guard separately with the toy company's security director and record the conversations. We wouldn't tell them about the PSE unless some evidence was turned up to warrant further questioning. That way no one would be offended.

We carefully formulated the questions and began interviewing each guard, which took almost three days. Between each interview, I would run the audio tapes through the PSE and see if anything looked out of place.

None of the guards showed any signs of stress except one- the field supervisor- our best man. Both the toy company and our guard company were very surprised and attributed this to nervousness. But I had been taught the machine can easily distinguish and account for nervous behavior, in fact that was why we asked the innocent non-important questions. This guy's non-pertinent questions showed little sign of stress or nervousness.

It was decided to interview him again; this time we would tell him we were using the PSE as a lie detector. I would have more freedom to ask baseline questions and try to target the cause of the stress. I would also restructure the questions to relieve as much stress as possible- for instance using the word "take", instead of "steal".

 When I asked him "Have you ever taken anything from _____ company "? The graph was dense- again indicating stress and possible untruthfulness.

Giving him every chance, I asked questions like, "Have you accidentally taken home property that didn't belong to you?"

Again, the graph indicated high stress. I explained to him what the machine was displaying. He denied any wrong doing; he denied stealing anything or taking anything.

The PSE results were too obvious and strong to ignore. The toy company's people wanted a resolution before they moved forward with others. It was finally agreed that we would ask him to allow us to search his home. If he refused, we would have no choice but to let him go. If he agreed and nothing was found, he would be cleared and nothing would ever be mentioned again.

He agreed and the toy company's security director and our manager went to his residence. I didn't go but I later learned nothing was found in his house at all. But, they noticed he had a detached garage, and when they looked through a window, saw boxes inside.

The guard refused to allow a search of the garage, so the police were called. They instructed him to open the door or they would obtain a search warrant because they could see what looked like part of the toy company's name on the boxes.

Our guard finally opened the garage door- and what they found stunned everyone. The garage was stacked from floor to ceiling with boxes of the secret action figures- thousands and thousands of them. I felt pretty bad and it made our company look bad but the PSE proved its worth beyond any doubt.

After doing a few little investigations with the PSE, which were non-conclusive, that is I never found out the final outcomes; I was called by Ron at American Alarm. Someone had damaged one of the cars and no one would own up to it.

It appeared someone had driven under a chain- likely by accident-, which scraped the hood, the roof, and the trunk- pretty badly. Ron thought they probably drove into a driveway by mistake and didn't see a chain across it in the dark. He was upset that five guys had access to the vehicle and no one would admit it or tell on whoever did do it.

With Ron standing next to me, I simply called each one of the service techs on the phone and asked if they knew anything about it- while warning them I was taping the conversation.

When I got to a service technician named Steve, the PSE immediately showed high stress. I asked him to come clean and he admitted he had been driving the car when it happened- case closed.

Another incident that really proved the worth of the PSE came as a result of an investigation at the bank that was owned by our parent company. A manager at one of the branches asked us to investigate a teller that continually came up short on her cash drawer.

The teller in question was black so the bank was leery of directly confronting her. We all decided that the best course would be to run everyone at the branch through the PSE. This way no one would be singled out. This time we were upfront with everyone that the PSE was in fact, a lie detector.

For an entire day, I interviewed all the tellers and mangers at that branch. Interestingly enough, the suspect teller came out clean and stress free; but one of the assistant managers did not!

I kept trying different approaches and questions and it just got worse.

"Have you ever taken anything from the bank?"

"No!" Result- high stress.

"Have you taken anything more than $10?"

"No, but I may have taken some pencils home". Result- high stress.

"Besides pencils or office supplies, have you ever taken anything more than $10 in value?"

Answer- "No!" Again -result high stress.

"Have you ever taken anything from the bank of more than $100 in value?"

Answer, "No!" Again- high stress.

I finally called the bank security department and told them I thought they had a big problem. They instructed me to leave and they would handle it. I found out later the Assistant Manager was gone and the black teller was still there.

Ultimately, I moved on to a different position (as you will read shortly) and was very relieved to leave behind the PSE. It was depressing to discover so many dishonest people.

Bob

After Terry's death, the management went on a search for a new service manager. The result was a guy named Bob. A fairly young, very easygoing man who I met the very first week he started work. Unlike Terry, Bob was determined to check in on each shift to see what was going on.

Bob & I hit it off at once. In fact, Bob hit it off with everyone- especially Geraldine, who instantly took a liking to him in a quiet sort of way.

Bob struggled to balance his responsibility as a manager with his love for fun and action. He wasn't as much an action junkie as Earl and I, but he did enjoy going on alarm runs. Often he would work all night and then pay the price in the morning- when he was actually supposed to be working.

Using the argument that most of the service happened at night, he got away with it for a while but John & Ron, (the president & vice president of American Alarm) finally insisted he spend more time on the day shift.

Even then, Bob frequently stayed over and he and I ran many alarms. Our relationship would grow as other events transpired, but suffice to say I liked him a lot and knew he was someone you could rely on.

Bob's style of management soon completely eliminated any friction between the Central Station and the Service department. Of course, it didn't hurt that he and I were friends; but I think one of the biggest factors was that he took an interest in Geraldine as well.

The Blizzard

After the hot summer, it seemed as though the winter was determined to make up for lost time. In January of 1978, Greater Cincinnati was hit with one of the worst blizzards in Ohio history.

Being Cincinnati, it couldn't just be snow- there had to be an ice component and it was really bad. The day before it had rained; cold and hard. The rain continued through the night until the temperature dropped and then froze. The rain turned to snow, which covered the ice.

When I awoke the following morning I saw the ground covered with a foot of snow. Without taking the time to listen to the news, I got in my car and backed out of my garage and onto the street.

Since I lived on a low hill, I had to drive down to get to the main road. At the bottom was a stop sign, which I planned on running so I wouldn't get stuck. It was a good plan but when I got to the bottom, the car kind of squirmed and shimmied from side to side.

I realized my car had actually fallen through a top sheet of ice and underneath was running water! The exposed water froze instantly since the temperature was now about 20 below zero.

Luckily, the Firebird V-8 had plenty of power and I was able to break free but I knew it was pointless to continue so I slammed it in reverse and backed up the hill to my driveway.

My driveway ran down into my garage and much too late I discovered the brakes covered in ice. I couldn't stop as the car slid all the way down the driveway and *though* the still closed garage door.

I had to live with a boarded up garage for a week until the weather broke and someone could come and fix it.

In the meantime, I called the office and told them I was stuck- along with everyone else. The police ordered all the roads closed and everyone was ordered to stay home.

The alarm business went on however. Good old Bob actually drove over and met me out on the main road where I had hiked out in what was now 14 inches of snow. Together we ran a bunch of service calls to try and take care of our customers. At one point my pants and boots were so wet they froze solid. I remember we stopped in and fixed the alarm at one of the industrial plants and I took the opportunity to visit their lunchroom and put my boots in their microwave to thaw them out.

The treacherous weather conditions lasted for over a week. The wind chill factor reached over 32 below zero. Once I was finally able to reach the Central Station, Bob and I spent a few nights there. My most memorable event was when we decided to go home.

Bob and I came down the stairs and out into the cold. Snow plows had piled about three feet of snow up in front of our building. As I walked by, I noticed a red knit glove sticking out of the snow pile. Bob reached down and touched it- and we realized it was on a hand!

A wino apparently had passed out sometime over night and probably froze to death and the snowplow had covered the body. We called the police but it took them nearly four hours to arrive. I made up my mind right then to leave Cincinnati as soon as I could and return to sunny California. Events would transpire however, that would keep me there for several more years.

Malcolm

People were forced to stay inside for almost two weeks. The term "Cabin Fever" was discussed on every newscast. American Alarm was running on skeleton shifts of operators working 12 and 16 hour shifts- only those who lived close could get in, even though the service guys were picking up and dropping off as many as they could. As if the weather wasn't enough to depress everyone, more bad news was on the way.

Malcolm, the English gentleman and Central Station Manager, had a heart attack while on duty. They carried him out on a stretcher and rushed him to the hospital where he passed away. That left quite a vacuum and no one knew what to do. Ron, the Vice President whose main responsibility was Sales and Operations seemed unable to deal with the situation and as a result, the Central Station was rudderless for the first time in twelve years.

The following week, I got a call from John, the president of American Alarm. Could I please come over and meet with him?

My first thought was something really bad happened that involved me. Maybe I had somehow missed a break in or I was being accused of something. Customers often called in and accused servicemen of silly little things like drinking someone's orange juice or stealing pens off someone's desk.

Instead he offered me the Central Station Manager job! John explained he thought highly of me, that I learned the business from the ground up, and that he was planning on introducing a new computer system into the operation and knew I had some experience. Finally, he thought I had real maturity and sense of responsibility because of my military duty.

Overnight, I went from peon to boss. I wish I had photos of the Central Station operator's faces when they found out I was now their manager. It was a stunning turnaround and a real opportunity for me.

The first week I learned why Malcolm had a heart attack. I was surprised he lasted as long as he did. The mostly female staff (and the gay guys acted just like women) drove me absolutely crazy with gossip, backbiting, menstrual periods, and general bitching. Many of them didn't show up for work either and I realized why Malcolm had so many people working there- to cover shifts for people that didn't want to work.

I pondered the situation and decided major changes were required. My first order of business was to get the no-shows under control. In a flash of brilliance (I must say), I rammed through a new pay scale.

Anyone who I determined was qualified to be a shift supervisor would automatically make an extra one dollar per hour- but, they would they then handle all the problems and be responsible for getting people to work.

That cured that problem, as the women pulled no punches when their shift operators didn't show up. After a few weeks of letting things settle down, I streamlined the schedule and got rid of most of the dead weight.

My next move was also controversial; I convinced John & Ron I needed an assistant. Not just a secretary but also a real assistant manager with power. If we were going to go computerized, we needed someone who was intelligent and had some initiative.

It was my choice that raised objections- Linda. But I truly felt she was the only one with enough brains and willingness to change and be successful and actually help me.

They reluctantly agreed (I had them over a barrel to some extent), but only to give her a chance. If she didn't work out, she would go back to being a part timer on the graveyard shift.

My next problem was to convince Linda! I never told her about their comments, I just said I was taking a risk but I felt she was the only one who could handle it.

Knowing she was a wife and mother of two school age kids, I knew it might be a hardship for her; to my surprise she immediately agreed to take the position.

The Computer from Hell

Within a few months, our new computer arrived- along with the developer and a technical crew. Back in the mid 70's, the term "computer" was used very loosely.

First of all, the state of the art was large- our computer was in a rack the size of a refrigerator. Secondly, two computers were required- one of them a backup. These "advanced" Data General machines had a grand total of 48 K of memory that's 48 thousand- not million!. The "hard drive" consisted of disks the size of garbage cans lids. One half was removable for backups. The machines were loaded via switches on the front panel.

The whole system including the software was a work in progress at best. It was much more art than science. The software was being developed as it was deployed. American Alarm was only the 13th alarm company in the world to attempt to go computerized.

Alarm monitoring at the time was very labor intensive. Not only did we have the thousands and thousands of "direct wire" alarms- with the meters, lights, & buzzers but another 5000 or so "McCullough Loops". These were multi-drop systems that transmitted telegraph like signals to a paper tape in the Central Station.

Loops were cost effective because many clients and locations could share the same telephone line. Each location or alarm device would have a transmitter that sent a coded signal.

The system was even more archaic than the direct wires. A spring wind up mechanism (yes, I said wind up) would turn a toothed wheel. As the wheel turned the teeth opened and closed the circuit and a pen at the Central Station that would mark a paper tape- almost like Morse code.

In order to give that transmitter a unique identity, some of the teeth on the code wheel were broken off. This would form the code that would be transmitted.

So, for example, to get a transmitter code of 333- teeth were broken off until all that was left was 3 teeth followed by a space and another 3 teeth, followed by a space and the last 3:

___XXX_XXX_XXX_____.

The operator at the Central Station would then be required to "read" the tape and hopefully figure out something that looked like this

_____|_|_|_____|_|_|_____|_|_|___ meant 333.

That operator would then look up 333 in a book and see who it was and what they were supposed to do.

Not only was there a lot of room for error in just interpreting those marks but having to take the time to look it up wasted valuable minutes. To make matters even worse, very often two or more transmitters sent signals at the same time causing a unreadable series of marks called a "clash".

The computer was supposed to relieve all this. It could count the signals and look up the location and display account information on a terminal screen- as well as do all the time stamps and record keeping.

No one would be reckless enough to switch over completely to the computer, so the old systems were left in place and a comparison was run for months until confidence built up in the computer.

When it worked, it was great. We quickly discovered that our two crack day shift operators- Shirley and Anne-Marie had really no idea what signals they were getting- they just assumed which customers were transmitting due to the time of day.

The computer disagreed with them almost 100% of the time. When we would compare the paper tapes against the computer, we could verify it was correct and thee humans were wrong. Naturally this caused an immense amount of friction between woman and machine.

But the women often prevailed simply because the computer was down more than it was up. The most frequent problem was "crashes". This term originates from those large disk drives. The flying read- write head of the drive would actually physically hit the surface of the disk if it encountered the tiniest dust particle, and wipe out all the data. It was a real crash- not just a minor inconvenience.

Consequently I spent most of my waking moments- sometimes 24 hours straight- working to keep these machines running. They required constant maintenance, housekeeping, tweaking, and software modifications.

Linda turned out to be my greatest idea. She pretty much ran the office while I worked on the computers. She was invaluable in every respect, and as a result gained everyone else's respect. I could not have survived without her. Not only was she great as an Assistant Manager but also as a sounding board, chaplain, secretary, friend, and a relief for sore eyes (she just looked so beautiful dressed in her business attire).

Over a period of time, I gained knowledge of the computers and software and learned many tricks to keep them at peak efficiency. All too frequently, the disk drives would record so many errors they would be unreadable. I suspected that, due to the random nature of this problem, that it was temperature related. A disk that was good in the morning often was unreadable later in the day. I hit on the idea of placing a bad disk in the freezer for about 20 minutes, and viola- it would be readable long enough to retrieve the data.

Of course, the company that provided the computer system told us that we were the only ones having such problems. I began calling around to the other 12 users and found they were even worse off than we were. This led to the formation of the Computerized Alarm Association, a user's group that met around the county at different user locations, to lobby the manufacturer to improve the system.

Soon after I was dealt a serious blow. John, the president, called me into his office and after swearing me to secrecy; said the company was being sold. The owner was over 70 and decided to liquidate all his assets. This shocked me to the core since this was my first real job and I had been there nearly ten years.

The first day of the next month Honeywell officially took over. Honeywell of course was a giant corporation and John told everyone it would bring great opportunities. It seemed good on the outside but I felt an underlying sense of unease.

Honeywell quickly began exerting their authority with procedures and paperwork. We were all slightly shocked that their processes so manual. Since Honeywell is a computer company we would have thought they are more advanced then us.

Steve, the Central Station Manager from Indianapolis, and I had been scheduled to fly to Los Angeles for a meeting of the Computerized Alarm Association. John told us to go ahead and finagled us an invitation to Honeywell's Research & Development center in Irvine, Ca.

It was really nice getting back to California but when we visited Honeywell, I was very under whelmed. Being a arrogant large corporation, Honeywell was not about to buy a computer system from a little guy; they were determined to develop their own. They hadn't gotten very far.

Honeywell's "system" was still in prototype stage and crashed often while we were there. It was crude to say the least. I left depressed-especially since they hinted we would have to use it since Honeywell wouldn't support any "outside" entity.

The Alarm Association meeting was being held at API (American Protection Industries) near downtown LA. By contrast when we went to the meeting it was obvious API was a cutting edge company. They had 6 offices all over southern California and were the largest security company in all of California.

While they were using the same computer system and basic software as us- they had a team of programmers modifying and improving it. The results- which we observed operating – were impressive and innovative.

API put on a huge dinner that evening and I had a chance to speak with most of the executives. It was apparent they were growing rapidly and hints were thrown around that they were always looking for good people.

My decision came very quickly. There was no longer anything to keep me in Cincinnati. I probably would have left a year before if I hadn't met Vickie. Now that she wasn't in my life- what difference did it make?

I reciprocated to API that I was always interested in being with a leader. A few days after we returned to Cincinnati, a letter arrived offering me a job. With a mixture of excitement and hesitation, I told John and Ron of my decision to leave.

Ron wasn't happy and accused me of using the trip to look for a job. John, on the other hand, while telling me I would do better at Honeywell at least was happy that I would be advancing somewhere.

Linda was the obvious choice for my replacement so I was able to arrange to leave for California in less than a month. I felt it was best to sever ties as quickly as possible.

Going Away

American Alarm threw a huge going away party for me at an exclusive restaurant. They really spared no expense and everyone was there.

My going away present was a photo album with pictures of everyone who worked at American Alarm. Some of them hated each other but still posed together for the picture. There was also a single photo of every single person. This is one of my most cherished possessions to this day. It contains the only pictures I have of Linda, Laura, Pam, and Vickie - women I had grown very close to at various periods.

By midnight everyone was pretty far gone, -especially Vickie who was completely out of it. While I was saying goodbye to John she came over and started handing me articles of her clothing to hold; first her coat, then her belt, then her purse. John gave us both a weird look but finally told me to take care of her.

Vickie asked me to take her home. I had no idea where her car was but I complied. It was so good being close to her again but I suppose she thought she was on safe ground since I was leaving the state!

When we got to her place, she immediately took off all her clothes and lay back on her bed nude. Beckoning me to her she said, "Make love to me one more time."

I got on the bed and began kissing her but almost immediately she passed out. It was the final blow but I laughed it off. Perhaps it was for the best. Fate stepped in to save me. I left quietly and went home to finish packing.

California

The very next morning I pointed my 1983 Mustang GT west and set out on a journey to a new life. I had three long days alone thinking of where I was coming from and where I was going. Yes, Vickie was on my mind nearly every mile.

Rolling into LA was like a new beginning. The sun was shining brightly and it was very warm for November. My spirits lifted. On the trip I had firmly set my mind to forget the past and look to the future.

My new job was Technical Support Manager- responsible for keeping all internal systems in operation- and kept me extremely busy. API, must like American, was owned by one of the richest men in California, if not the country. He owned skyscrapers and malls and Teleflora. He had rich and powerful friends. API provided security to all of them including many Hollywood stars.

Most impressive was their cutting edge technology. API had already mostly phased out the old "Direct Wire" and "McCullough Loops" and was transitioning to new Digital Dialers and Multiplex . Everything was computerized and I learned so much the first month my head was spinning.

Just traveling around to their branch offices was a daunting task. With Central Stations in Los Angeles, Hollywood, Van Nuys, Pomona, Orange County, and San Diego I was always on the go. A new headquarters in Culver City was in the process of being built so I had to be there almost every day.

A guy named Ron was the project manager there and we'd finish up late each evening by having a drink from a bottle he kept in his desk.

API at the Cutting Edge

Although there was a huge hole in my private life, my job at API kept my mind off it to a large degree. The new headquarters at Culver City was nearing completion and involved a huge amount of work setting up the generators, computers, security, and especially the Central Station.

This new Central Station was unlike anything anyone had ever seen. Direct wires and loops were no where in sight- everything was totally automated and computerized. The operators even dialed the phone through their computer.

The room was quiet and subdued with low lighting and comfortable chairs since the operators no longer had to run around the room.

I was very proud of the building; it was a showcase of the industry. Of all the Central Stations around the country I had visited over the years, this was so far above the norm it set a new standard.

Because my job was very visible anyway and with the success of the new building, I began advancing rapidly through the ranks. My first promotion was to the Director of Engineering and our first task was to work with manufacturers to develop custom products.

API had such large buying power we were able to specify exactly what we wanted. John, our new Product Development manger, and I went after our biggest false alarm and service problem first: motion detectors.

We worked with a company called Detection Systems and jointly developed a new type of passive infrared. A radical part of the formula was to have every detector burned in and tested before delivery so we could assure ourselves of no out of the box failures. This cost a little more but we convinced management that if we could save the cost of one service call we would more than make up the difference.

The new DS Motion detectors proved very successful so we applied our knowledge and experience to other products. The biggest challenge was a complete new alarm control panel. Up till this time, companies used different panels for intrusion, high security, residential, commercial and fire. Working with a company named Digital Monitoring Products (DMP) we developed one advanced control panel that could do all systems by interchanging modules. Eventually, the hardware would be replaced by software and through programming the panel would take on different tasks.

This same company helped us develop new intelligent keypads that were the first to use English language displays- another radical departure from LEDs that did not provide any feedback.

As part of this program, API's keypads were private labeled- an industry first. We even had them made in black so they wouldn't show dirt and look good much longer.

API was the very first security company to use color CCTV surveillance cameras. Color provides much more "information" such as the color of a suspect's clothes Up to then however, color was considered prohibitively expensive. I knew that this was strictly a function of manufacturing supply and demand.

Again we convinced management and sales that color was the better way to go. Other security companies thought we were crazy but the customers loved color and were willing to pay extra and as sales quantities grew, the cost started falling.

Customer service was one more area where API set itself apart. We were the only security company to employ a full time customer service department and major accounts representatives. API didn't just pay lip service to this but had a staff of over a dozen full time customer service personnel who actively visited customers, solved problems- and reaped the benefits of additional services.

Standout Projects

API had customers from major defense contactors to large shopping malls to extravagant mansions. I was exposed to every type of system and at one time or another was called in to fix some problem that had eluded everyone else.

My lack of fear served me well on some of these occasions. Once we were called on the carpet at General Dynamics- a huge manufacturer of naval weapons in Pomona. The fire alarm API recently installed was not functioning and the executive threatened to throw us out- along with the $100,000 they owed us.

The president of API asked me to go to the meeting with him. Before we went in, I made a quick check of the panel and saw a particular warning light on.

The meeting was not going well. Not only were they threatening to cancel the contract but were going to sue us for negligence. Finally, I piped up and told them I could have the system up and operating within three hours. (I just said three because I didn't want to make it sound too easy- I really thought I could do it in an hour or less).

Bill, the president of API, looked at me like I was crazy but went along with it. He told them I was the foremost expert on this fire system in the United States. The GD executives agreed to give me three hours and we would reconvene the following day.

When Bill got me outside, he asked if I was sane. I assured him I could do it to which he commented something like :"*You have the biggest balls I've ever seen...*"

I went right to work and sure enough my hunch was correct. There was a ground strap missing between the fire panels many cabinets. This was causing an erroneous ground fault. In defense of the installers, the ground strap requirement was not clearly documented. But I knew about it from our tests in the development lab and was the president's hero after that.

But the all time most interesting project had to be the "Malibu house". This was a radical mansion being built near the beach in Malibu by an unknown doctor. The radical part was that is was costing over 25 million dollars and was constructed completely from poured concrete!

The doctor apparently had a hang up about "angles" so he dictated that no angles could appear anywhere in the house-only curves were permitted. Nor could there be any window or door frames. He wanted glass to appear "floating and doors to look as if they were hanging in mid air. This necessitated that every single aspect of the house had to be custom made.

Such a project called for a radical security system and along with the sales rep Joe, we designed the most cutting edge system of it's time. In fact, the system stood as a cut above anything else available for many years afterwards.

The project consumed three years. Products that were originally sold became obsolete and newer technology was substituted. Every device had to be carefully planned as to its location so the necessary space could be allowed for in the concrete pours which went on for over a year.

The architect and interior decorator were constantly involved in our design and both had veto power over anything. So every decision had to be run by one of them. One controlled the outside, the other the inside. Nothing could be painted for instance; every metal surface had to be either copper plated or anodized black.

We designed a system where the doctor could use his personal access card at a reader outside in the driveway and all the gates and doors assigned to him would automatically unlock, disarm the corresponding alarms, and turn on the proper area light if it was dark.

Over twenty cameras were fed into a graphic map of the property and the home television system. You could put any TV in the house to a certain channel and then press a button on the map to see the camera view- or the camera would pop up automatically if an intrusion was detected in that area.

API even installed a telephone system which could control any of the gates so the doctor could see and talk to a visitor at any of the gates and then let them in by pressing a button on the phone.

The crowning touch for me was the "beach alarm". In California, the beaches are public by law; but the doctor wanted to know if someone was on "his" section of the beach. The difficulty was that his beach access was quite a ways from the house and down stairs cut into the side of a cliff.

It was just impossible to run wires down the side of the cliff so we came up with beams powered by solar cells which transmitted alarm signals wirelessly to the main house alarm panel. The finishing touch was a voice announcement that warned people they were trespassing if they crossed through the beam.

Just as the system and the house were finally completed, a huge scandal erupted over the doctor's business. It turned out he made all his money running blood testing labs but unfortunately, his employees often failed to actually perform these tests!

We all probably should have suspected something when the doctor insisted on two inch thick bullet glass on the ocean facing windows.

The finished house was tied up in litigation for many years but still exists hidden away off a road in Malibu and Joe and I are very proud of what we were able to accomplish.

Hollywood

Due to its reputation, - and proximity to Hollywood, API was very active in filmmaking. We often got requests to consult on security devices in movies and frequently lent equipment to film crews. Since I was the Engineering Manager, it mostly came down to me to handle these requests. On several occasions I went to the studio and set up card readers and cameras for filming.

The humorous aspect was that state of the art technology did not appeal to art directors and directors. They wanted older equipment such as large cameras, which stood out instead of the newer ones, which were much smaller and more discreet.

One movie called for quite a few card readers that the hero would have to use to gain entrance to a "secret" facility. The new generation of card readers were proximity- meaning a card merely had to get close to a sealed reader for it to function. The director hated that- he wanted readers which required the card be inserted because it looked better. I had to dig through obsolete equipment in storage to come up with enough to make the movie.

API's closeness to Hollywood also translated into business with movie stars as well. The actual names and numbers were too numerous to mention but one in particular stands out.

In 1990 the sales department got a call from a Ms. Ciccone about some cameras. The lead was turned over to our CCTV specialist Arnie who then called me. Ciccone was Madonna's last name and Arnie knew I was a big fan. An appointment was made and the following day I arrived at a modern Hollywood Hills home.

Expecting a huge meeting, I rang the doorbell and was greeted by a short woman with brown hair who led me into the home where she then sat behind a desk. It was only at that moment I realized it was Madonna. She was much shorter than expected and had dyed her hair for a movie.

This was at the early height of her popularity and despite her millions you could not have asked for a less pretentious person. She was matter of fact and down to earth. I secured the job and the following weeks spent much time there with our installation crew to make sure everything went well.

During this time, I discovered Madonna's work ethic. She would rise very early each morning and do a brutal two- three hour workout followed by a bike ride in the hills. Then she would return and work on her music for the rest of the day.

A few days into the job, we were also rewarded with the presence of another huge movie star. Early one morning who should walk out of Madonna's bedroom but Warren Beatty!

Amusingly, he would have none of her workouts but was completely genuine and friendly. Coming up to each of us, he shook hands and said "Hi, I'm Warren."

Although it was humorous (as if we didn't know who he was), it came across as extremely friendly. He would then ask us politely what we were doing and then leave Madonna to her exercise.

Madonna was also a tough businesswoman. I had suggested a certain level of security for the home but she thought this was too much and cut back- a whole $6000. A month or so later someone climbed up the hill in back of her home and walked in and stole her address book. She promptly called me back to install the extra security.

A few weeks later I got a autographed picture in the mail with the inscription "Yo, Ed!"

I still have it.

The following year, API obtained the security contract for Warner Brother's studios. I began spending a great deal of time there and met many more stars. During the installation we would see all kinds of celebrities walking around and working. Mel Gibson happened to drive in almost every day, but this was supposed to be a very secret event since a Gay Right's group was after him for some reason.

The Best Years

During the 1990s, API was at its peak. I moved through several jobs and then set up a new Engineering department, which supported Sales in complex proposals such as Warner Brothers.

Part of the perks of working at API and with sales, were the annual trips to sales meetings. One year it was a resort in Phoenix, then San Diego. But the highlight was Maui! Yes we were sent to Maui for an all expense paid trip for a week. We had to attend one meeting, which was also an awards dinner, and then we were on our own.

We were all on top of the world but in a case of deja vue, the owner decided to liquidate all his assets to acquire another huge company. API was promptly sold to a British security firm called Modern Alarm. This turned out to be a blessing since Modern was even more cutting edge than API. Once the two companies began to understand each other and realize what we had, there started much cross-pollination of ideas.

The best part was the trips to England. The first time we spent ten days there just before Christmas. We were taken all over to visit Modern's various offices and entities. One night I even rode in a Rolls Royce and talked to friends back in the U.S on one of the first cell phones while we sped down the M5 at about 100 miles per hour. I fell in love with the country and have been back many times.

We quickly discovered on these trips just how advanced Modern was and brought back all kinds of new technology. API had been reforming itself into a "Loss Prevention" company and Modern fit in with this concept perfectly. They had developed "Cash Register Monitoring"; a system to detect employee theft in retail.

Once we returned back to California, I was tasked to develop a similar system for API to market. The concept involved analyzing transaction data from the cash registers in conjunction with video cameras and recordings.

Employees, it turns out, are incredibly ingenious when it comes to discovering ways to steal. I quickly learned employee theft accounts for up to 87% of business losses. If API could save even a fraction of this loss, the system would pay for itself and we would reap the profits.

Target Stores was one of API's customers at the time and we learned a great deal from observing their store operations. At one location we were installing alarm contacts at the receiving area and I was there to make sure the installation was going well and to gather feedback on techniques and device.

As I was speaking with one of the assistant managers, an employee rolled a large trash bin piled high with debris past us. The manager noticed something and stopped the employee. As I watched, she lifted some of the empty cardboard up and underneath were brand new items from the store!

The manager explained some dishonest employees would simply take inventory off the shelves, pretend to throw it away as defective and then return after the store closed and get it out of the trash.

I immediately called our account rep for Target, who then called the Security Director. That Assistant Manager was promoted and API got to install cameras and alarms on the trash dumpsters- at additional extra profit.

Although we have seen videotapes of employees simply taking money out of the register and putting it in their pocket, this was actually extremely rare because it was so easily detectable.

The more sophisticated thieves found ways around the systems. POS (Point of Sale) and barcode scanners were supposed to eliminate theft and mistakes. In effect they often made it much easier and harder to discover.

A favorite trick was for the cashier to invite friends and relatives to shop in their stores while they were working the checkout. The accomplice would then bring high-ticket items- such as cigarettes or liquor, to their checkout. The dishonest employee would then pretend to scan the item but instead scan a barcode they had stashed somewhere- like on their watchband. The bogus barcode would be from a pack of gum or something- so the transaction would show a sale of 10 cents or a dollar.

Once we figured out what was happening we would modify our software to detect these events. For example, any POS checkout showing multiple 10-cent transactions would trigger a flag so store security could then check the video recording and see what transpired.

At another retail chain, our system uncovered a significant money-laundering ring because we ran a report of all cash transactions over $100. One store showed 900 in one day!

The Loss Prevention experience and working with Modern Alarm was the high point of my career. It was always challenging, interesting and different. And we saved our customers money to boot.

Change Is Not Necessarily Good

Of course, such good fortune just couldn't last. Modern was so successful it attracted a group of investors who leveraged the company and ran it into the ground- along with API. Our cash reserves were drained and sent overseas.

Tottering on the verge of bankruptcy, API was sold to ADT- the world's largest- and worst security company. I stuck it out there for a year but ADT was only interested in making their numbers look good. They dismantled all the cherished Customer Service departments as being too expensive and moved all the monitoring operations to Denver. API's old customers left in droves.

ADT was inefficient, disorganized and greedy. ADT was owned by Tyco and the subsequent scandal proved my point.

In 1998 I had an opportunity to help start a new security company which was formed to take over the business of one of API's largest former customers. Although it was interesting, the job lacked the challenges of the previous years.

As I write this, alarm and security technology is completely unlike it was when I started. Digital video is all the rage and security delves deeply into the IT or Information Technology world.

I kind of miss those lights and buzzers sometimes..........

About the author

Ed Morawski has been involved with electronics since his teens. After joining the U.S. Air Force in 1966 he was trained as an Aircraft Instrument Technician and spent the next eight years working on every aircraft in the inventory on bases from Langley AFB, VA. to Vietnam and finally at Edwards AFB, CA.

After receiving an Honorable Discharge he began working as a technician for American Alarm Company in Cincinnati, OH. He become manager of the central station and worked there for ten years until the company was acquired by Honeywell Alarm.

Mr. Morawski moved to Los Angeles in 1983 and became Technical Support Manager for API, the largest security company in California. Over the next 13 years he held various positions such as Applications Manager, Director of Engineering and Sales Support Manager. API was acquired by ADT in 1996 and Mr. Morawski became Regional Installation Manager and later Western Region Manager for the Engineered Systems Division.

In 1998 Mr. Morawski helped start UPS Security, which was primarily involved in remote management of security systems for the Irvine Company and 300 other large customers. He helped developed several unique services and systems for customers such as Memorial Care Hospitals and the City Of San Diego.

Mr. Morawski also started Hi-Tech-Consulting.com in 2005 to assist small business customers in obtaining electronic security systems utilizing the very latest technology and thinking. He currently runs Edge Security Systems Inc in Southern California.

www.ingramcontent.com/pod-product-compliance
Lightning Source LLC
Chambersburg PA
CBHW070642290526
45790CB00001B/170